Cram101 Textbook Outlines to accompany:

Child Welfare and Family Services: Policies and Practice

Susan Whitelaw Downs, 8th Edition

A Cram101 Inc. publication (c) 2010.

PRACTICE EXAMS.

Get all of the self-teaching practice exams for each chapter of this textbook at **www.Cram101.com** and ace the tests. Here is an example:

Chapter 1

Child Welfare and Family Services: Policies and Practice
Susan Whitelaw Downs, 8th Edition,
All Material Written and Prepared by Cram101

I WANT A BETTER GRADE.   Items 1 - 50 of 100.

1 A _____ consists of a domestic group of people, typically affiliated by birth or marriage, or by analogous or comparable relationships — including domestic partnership, cohabitation, adoption, surname and ownership.

  ○ Family   ○ Facadism
  ○ Face value   ○ Face-ism

2 A _____ is a boy or girl who has not reached puberty, but also refers to offspring of any age.

  ○ Child   ○ C. R. Boxer
  ○ Cabinet collective responsibility   ○ Cables Wynd House

3 _____ is the legal act of permanently placing a child with a parent or parents other than the birth mother or father. An _____ order has the effect of severing the parental responsibilities and rights of the birth parents and transferring those responsibilities and rights onto the adoptive parents.

  ○ Adoption   ○ Aarne-Thompson classification system
  ○ Aaron Lynch   ○ Abacus School

4 _____ is a system by which a certified, stand-in "parent" cares for minor children or young peoples who have been removed from their birth parents or other custodial adults by state authority. Responsibility for the young person is assumed by the relevant governmental authority and a placement with another family found. There can be voluntary placements by a parent of a child into _____.

  ○ Foster care   ○ Facadism
  ○ Face value   ○ Face-ism

You get a 50% discount for the online exams. Go to **Cram101.com**, click Sign Up at the top of the screen, and enter DK73DW9304 in the promo code box on the registration screen. Access to Cram101.com is $4.95 per month, cancel at any time.

With Cram101.com online, you also have access to extensive reference material.

You will nail those essays and papers. Here is an example from a Cram101 Biology text:

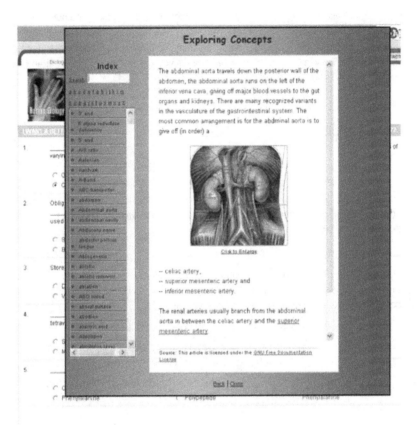

Learning System

Cram101 Textbook Outlines is a learning system. The notes in this book are the highlights of your textbook, you will never have to highlight a book again.

How to use this book. Take this book to class, it is your notebook for the lecture. The notes and highlights on the left hand side of the pages follow the outline and order of the textbook. All you have to do is follow along while your instructor presents the lecture. Circle the items emphasized in class and add other important information on the right side. With Cram101 Textbook Outlines you'll spend less time writing and more time listening. Learning becomes more efficient.

Cram101.com Online

Increase your studying efficiency by using Cram101.com's practice tests and online reference material. It is the perfect complement to Cram101 Textbook Outlines. Use self-teaching matching tests or simulate in-class testing with comprehensive multiple choice tests, or simply use Cram's true and false tests for quick review. Cram101.com even allows you to enter your in-class notes for an integrated studying format combining the textbook notes with your class notes.

Visit **www.Cram101.com**, click Sign Up at the top of the screen, and enter **DK73DW9304** in the promo code box on the registration screen. Access to www.Cram101.com is normally $9.95 per month, but because you have purchased this book, your access fee is only $4.95 per month. Sign up and stop highlighting textbooks forever.

Child Welfare and Family Services: Policies and Practice
Susan Whitelaw Downs, 8th

CONTENTS

Chapter 1. An Introduction to Family and Child Services

Family	A family consists of a domestic group of people, typically affiliated by birth or marriage, or by analogous or comparable relationships — including domestic partnership, cohabitation, adoption, surname and ownership.
Child	A child is a boy or girl who has not reached puberty, but also refers to offspring of any age.
Adoption	Adoption is the legal act of permanently placing a child with a parent or parents other than the birth mother or father. An adoption order has the effect of severing the parental responsibilities and rights of the birth parents and transferring those responsibilities and rights onto the adoptive parents.
Foster care	Foster care is a system by which a certified, stand-in "parent" cares for minor children or young peoples who have been removed from their birth parents or other custodial adults by state authority. Responsibility for the young person is assumed by the relevant governmental authority and a placement with another family found. There can be voluntary placements by a parent of a child into foster care.
Purpose	Purpose in its most general sense is the anticipated aim which guides action. It is used as the synonym of "goal" and "objective."
Role	A role or a social role is a set of connected behaviors, rights and obligations as conceptualized by actors in a social situation. It is an expected behavior in a given individual social status and social position. It is vital to both functionalist and interactionist understandings of society.
Social role	A social role is a set of connected behaviors, rights and obligations as conceptualized by actors in a social situation. It is mostly defined as an expected behavior in a given individual social status and social position.
Welfare	Welfare is financial assistance paid by taxpayers to people who are unable to support themselves. Some welfare is general, while specific and can only be invoked under certain circumstances, such as a scholarship. Individuals may apply for welfare due to disability, lack of education or job training, a low demand for unskilled labor, substance abuse, or an unwillingness to work.
Hurricane	A hurricane is one of many meteorological terms for a storm system characterized by a low pressure center and thunderstorms that produces strong wind and flooding rain. It feeds on the heat released when moist air rises and the water vapor it contains condenses.
Hurricane Katrina	Hurricane Katrina was the costliest and one of the five deadliest hurricanes in the history of the United States. It was the sixth-strongest Atlantic hurricane ever recorded and the third-strongest hurricane on record that made landfall in the United States. Katrina formed on August 23 during the 2005 Atlantic hurricane season and caused devastation along much of the north-central Gulf Coast. The most severe loss of life and property damage occurred in New Orleans, Louisiana, which flooded as the levee system catastrophically failed, in many cases hours after the storm had moved inland.

Population	A population is the collection of people or organisms of a particular species living in a given geographic area or space, usually measured by a census.
Generation	Generation is the act of producing offspring. It can also refer to the act of creating something inanimate such as electrical generation or cryptographic code generation.
Minority	A minority is a sociological group that does not constitute a politically dominant plurality of the total population of a given society. A sociological minority is not necessarily a numerical minority it may include any group that is disadvantaged with respect to a dominant group in terms of social status, education, employment, wealth and political power.
Internet	The Internet is a global system of interconnected computer networks that interchange data by packet switching using the standardized Internet Protocol Suite. It is a "network of networks" that consists of millions of private and public, academic, business, and government networks of local to global scope that are linked by copper wires, fiber-optic cables, wireless connections, and other technologies. The Internet carries various information resources and services, such as electronic mail, online chat, file transfer and file sharing, online gaming, and the inter-linked hypertext documents and other resources of the World Wide Web.
Lanham Act	The Lanham Act is a piece of legislation that contains the federal statutes of trademark law in the United States.
Mother	A mother is a biological and/or social female parent of an offspring. In the case of a mammal such as a human, the biological mother gestates a fertilized ovum, which is called first an embryo, and then a fetus. This gestation occurs in the mother"s uterus from conception until the fetus is sufficiently developed to be born. The mother then goes into labor and gives birth. Once the child is born, the mother produces milk in a process called lactation to feed the child; often the mother"s breast milk is the child"s sole nourishment for the first year or more of the child"s life.
Single-parent	A Single-parent is a parent who cares for children without the assistance of another person in the home. The legal definition of "single parenthood" may vary according to the local laws of different nations or regions.
Cultural diversity	Cultural diversity is the variety of human societies or cultures in a specific region, or in the world as a whole.
Experience	Experience as a general concept comprises knowledge of or skill in or observation of some thing or some event gained through involvement in or exposure to that thing or event. The history of the word experience aligns it closely with the concept of experiment.
Organization	In sociology organization is understood as planned, coordinated and purposeful action of human beings to construct or compile a common tangible or intangible product or service.

Sacred Contagion	Sacred Contagion is the belief that spiritual properties within an object, place place usually by direct contact or physical proximity. While the concept of Sacred Contagion has existed in numerous cultures since before recorded history, the term "Sacred Contagion" originated with French sociologist Émile Durkheim, who introduced it in his book The Elementary Forms of Religious Life. An example of Sacred Contagion is chapters 11 through 15 in the Book of Leviticus found in the Bible and Torah.
Risk	Risk is a concept that denotes the precise probability of specific eventualities. Technically, the notion of Risk is independent from the notion of value and, as such, eventualities may have both beneficial and adverse consequences. However, in general usage the convention is to focus only on potential negative impact to some characteristic of value that may arise from a future event.
Single parent	A single parent is a parent who cares for one or more children without the assistance of another parent in the home. The legal definition may vary according to the local laws of different nations or regions.
Statistics	Statistics is a mathematical science pertaining to the collection, analysis, interpretation, and presentation of data. It is applicable to a wide variety of academic disciplines, from the physical and social sciences to the humanities; it is also used and misused for making informed decisions in all areas of business and government.
Status	In sociology or anthropology, social status is the honor or prestige attached to one"s position in society one"s social position. The stratification system, which is the system of distributing rewards to the members of society, determines social status. Social status, the position or rank of a person or group within the stratification system, can be determined two ways. One can earn their social status by their own achievements, which is known as achieved status, or one can be placed in the stratification system by their inherited position, which is called ascribed status.
Alienation	In sociology and critical social theory, alienation refers to an individual"s estrangement from traditional community and others in general. It is considered by many that the atomism of modern society means that individuals have shallower relations with other people than they would normally. This, it is argued, leads to difficulties in understanding and adapting to each other"s uniqueness see normlessness. It is also sometimes referred to as commodification, emphasizing the compatibility of capitalism with alienation a common theme of the early work of Karl Marx; see Marx"s theory of alienation.
Homelessness	Homelessness is the condition and societal category of people who lack housing and food, usually because they cannot afford a regular, safe, and adequate shelter. The term "homelessness" may also include people whose primary nighttime residence is in a homeless shelter, in an institution that provides a temporary residence for individuals intended to be institutionalized, or in a public or private place not designed for use as a regular sleeping accommodation for human beings.

Violence	*Violence* is the exertion of force with the intent to injure (psychologically or physically) or kill. *Violence* is also used more broadly and metaphorically to describe the destructive action of natural phenomena like storms and earthquakes. Variant uses of the term refer to the destruction of non-living objects
African Americans	African Americans are citizens or residents of the United States whose ancestors, usually in predominant part, were indigenous to Sub-Saharan Africa. Most are the descendants of captive Africans who were enslaved within the boundaries of the present United States.
Intravenous	Intravenous literally means into a vein and is mostly used as a route of administration of medication with the help of an injection directly into the vein: an intravenous injection.
Substance abuse	Substance abuse refers to the overindulgence in and dependence on a psychoactive leading to effects that are detrimental to the individual"s physical health or mental health, or the welfare of others.
Suicide	Suicide is the act of intentionally taking one"s own life. The term "suicide" can also be used as a noun to refer to a person who has killed himself or herself.
White people	White people is a term which is usually used to refer to human beings characterized, at least in part, by the light pigmentation of their skin. It often refers narrowly to people claiming ancestry exclusively from Europe. A broadly corresponding concept was the Caucasian race.
Drug	A drug is any chemical or biological substance, synthetic or non-synthetic, that when taken into the organism"s body, will in some way alter the functions of that organism. This broad definition can be taken to include such substances as food.
Convention	A convention is a set of agreed, stipulated or generally accepted social norms, norms, standards or criteria, often taking the form of a custom.
Court	A court is a public forum used by a power base to adjudicate disputes and dispense civil, labor, administrative and criminal justice under its laws. In common law and civil law states, courts are the central means for dispute resolution, and it is generally understood that all persons have an ability to bring their claims before a court. Similarly, those accused of a crime have the right to present their defense before a court.
Legal rights	Legal rights refrain from doing something or to obtain or refrain from obtaining an action, thing or recognition in civil society. Compare with duty, referring to behavior that is expected or required of the citizen, and with privilege, referring to something that can be conferred and revoked.
Nation	A Nation is a body of people who share a real or imagined common history, culture, language or ethnic origin, who typically inhabit a particular country or territory. The development and conceptualization of the Nation is closely related to the development of modern industrial states and Nation alist movements in Europe in the 18th and 19th centuries, although Nation alists would trace Nation s into the past along an uninterrupted lines of historical narrative.

Benedict Anderson argued that Nation s were "imagined communities" because "the members of even the smallest Nation will never know most of their fellow-members, meet them, or even hear of them, yet in the minds of each lives the image of their communion", and traced their origins back to vernacular print journalism, which by its very nature was limited with linguistic zones and addressed a common audience.

Right

In jurisprudence and law, a right is the legal or moral entitlement to do or refrain from doing something or to obtain or refrain from obtaining an action, thing or recognition in civil society. Compare with privilege, or a thing to which one has a just claim. They serve as rules of interaction between people, and, as such, they place constraints and obligations upon the actions of individuals or groups.

Court of last resort

In some countries, provinces and states, the court of last resort is the highest court whose rulings cannot be challenged.

United Nations

The United Nations is an international organization whose stated aims are to facilitate cooperation in international law, international security, economic development, social progress and human rights issues.

Online

The terms online and offline have specific meanings with respect to computer technology and telecommunication. The concepts have however been extended from their computing and telecommunication meanings into the area of human interaction and conversation, such that even offline can be used in contrast to the common usage of online.
In computer technology and telecommunication, online and offline are defined by Federal Standard 1037C.

Privacy

Privacy has no definite boundaries and it has different meanings for different people. It is the ability of an individual or group to keep their lives and personal affairs out of public view, or to control the flow of information about themselves.

Community

A community is a social group of organisms sharing an environment, normally with shared interests. In human communities, intent, belief, resources, preferences, needs, risks and a number of other conditions may be present and common, affecting the identity of the participants and their degree of cohesiveness.

Constitution

A constitution is a system, often codified as a written document, that establishes the rules and principles that govern an organization or political entity. In the case of countries, this term refers specifically to a national constitution defining the fundamental political principles, and establishing the structure, procedures, powers and duties, of a government.

National Historic Landmark	A National Historic Landmark is a building, site, structure, object that is officially recognized by the United States government for its historical significance. All National Historic Landmark s are listed in the National Register of Historic Places. Out of more than 80,000 places on the National Register, however, only about 2,430 are National Historic Landmark s.
Eighth Amendment	The Eighth Amendment Amendment VIII to the United States Constitution, which is part of the United States Bill of Rights, prohibits excessive bail or fines, as well as cruel and unusual punishment. The phrases employed are taken from the English Bill of Rights. The Cruel and Unusual Punishment Clause is the only part of the Amendment that has been made applicable to the states via the Due Process Clause of the Fourteenth Amendment. The Excessive Bail and Excessive Fines Clauses have not been made applicable to the states.
Fifth Amendment	The Fifth Amendment Amendment V of the United States Constitution, which is part of the Bill of Rights, is related to legal procedure. Its guarantees stem from English common law as established by Magna Carta in 1215. For instance, grand juries and the phrase "due process" both trace their origin to the Magna Carta.
First Amendment	The First Amendment to the United States Constitution is a part of the United States Bill of Rights that expressly prohibits the United States Congress from making laws "respecting an establishment of religion" or that prohibit free exercise of religion, laws that infringe the freedom of speech, infringe the freedom of the press, limit the right to peaceably assemble, or limit the right to petition the government for a redress of grievances.
Fourteenth Amendment	The Fourteenth Amendment Amendment XIV to the United States Constitution is one of the post-Civil War amendments known as the Reconstruction Amendments, first intended to secure rights for former slaves. It includes the Due Process and Equal Protection Clauses, among others. It was proposed on June 13, 1866, and was ratified on July 9, 1868. It is perhaps the most significant structural change to the Constitution since the passage of the United States Bill of Rights.
Fourth Amendment	The Fourth Amendment to the United States Constitution is one of the provisions included in the Bill of Rights. The Fourth Amendment guards against unreasonable searches and seizures, and was designed as a response to the controversial writs of assistance, which were a significant factor behind the American Revolution. Toward that end, the amendment specifies that judicially sanctioned search and arrest warrants must be supported by probable cause and be limited in scope according to specific information supplied by a person who has sworn by it and is therefore accountable to the issuing court.
Minnesota	Minnesota is a state located in the Midwestern region of the United States of America. The twelfth-largest state by area in the U.S., it is the 21st most populous, with just over five million residents as of 2006. Minnesota was carved out of the eastern half of the Minnesota Territory and admitted to the Union as the 32nd state on May 11, 1858. The state is known as the "Land of 10,000 Lakes," and those lakes and the other waters for which the state is named, together with state and national forests and parks, offer residents and tourists a vigorous outdoor lifestyle.

School	A school is an institution where students learn while under the supervision of teachers. In most systems of formal education, students progress through a series of schools: primary school, secondary school, and possibly a university or vocational school. A school may also be dedicated to one particular field, such as a school of economics or a school of dance.
Sixth Amendment	The Sixth Amendment Amendment VI of the United States Constitution sets forth rights related to criminal prosecutions in federal courts. The Supreme Court has ruled that the principal rights guaranteed by this amendment are so fundamental and important that they are also protected in state proceedings by the Fourteenth Amendment"s Due Process Clause.
United States	The United States is a constitutional federal republic comprising fifty states and a federal district. The country is situated mostly in central North America, where its forty-eight contiguous states and Washington, D.C., the capital district, lie between the Pacific and Atlantic Oceans, bordered by Canada to the north and Mexico to the south.
Abortion	An abortion is the removal or expulsion of an embryo or fetus from the uterus, resulting in or caused by its death. This can occur spontaneously as a miscarriage or be artificially induced by chemical, surgical or other means.
Minor	In law, the term minor is used to refer to a person who is under the age in which one legally assumes adulthood and is legally granted rights afforded to adults in society. Depending on the jurisdiction and application, this age may vary, but is usually marked at either 18 or 21. Specifically, the status of "minor" is defined by the age of majority[
Reproductive rights	Reproductive rights are rights relating to reproduction and reproductive health. Various reproductive rights have been claimed as human rights in international human rights documents, particularly with the ratification of the Convention to End Discrimination Against Women, and the adoption of the the Cairo Programme and the Beijing Platform. Reproductive rights are often held to include the right to legal abortion, the right to control one"s reproductive functions, the right to access quality reproductive healthcare, and the right to education and access in order to make reproductive choices free from coercion, discrimination, and violence.
Pierce v. Society of Sisters	Pierce v. Society of Sisters of the Holy Names of Jesus and Mary, 268 U.S. 510 (1925), was an early 20th century United States Supreme Court decision which significantly expanded coverage of the Due Process Clause in the Fourteenth Amendment to the United States Constitution. The case has been cited as a precedent in over 100 Supreme Court cases, including Roe v. Wade, 410 U.S. 113 (1973), as well as in more than 70 cases in the courts of appeals. After World War I, some states concerned about the influence of immigrants and "foreign" values looked to public schools for help.
Society	A society is a grouping of individuals, which is characterized by common interest and may have distinctive culture and institutions.

Child labor	Child labor is the employment of children under an age determined by law or custom. This practice is considered exploitative by many countries and international organizations. Child labor was not seen as a problem throughout most of history, only becoming a disputed issue with the beginning of universal schooling and the concepts of laborers and children"s rights.
City	A city is an urban area with a large population and a particular administrative, legal, or historical status.
Father	The father is defined as the male parent of an offspring. The adjective "paternal" refers to father, parallel to "maternal" for mother. According to the anthropologist Maurice Godelier, the parental role assumed by human males is a critical difference between human society and that of humans" closest biological relatives - chimpanzees and bonobos - who appear to be unaware of their "father" connection.
Illinois	The State of Illinois is a state of the United States of America, the 21st to be admitted to the Union. Illinois is the most populous state in the Midwest and the fifth most populous in the nation, and has a large and cosmopolitan population. Its balance of vast suburbs and the great metropolis of Chicago in the northeast, rural areas, small industrial cities, and renowned agricultural productivity in central and western Illinois, and the coal mines of the south give it a highly diverse economic base. Its central location, connecting the Great Lakes to the Mississippi River via the Illinois River, made it a transportation hub for 150 years. It is this mixture of factory and farm, of urban and rural, that makes Illinois a microcosm of the United States. An Associated Press analysis of 21 demographic factors determined Illinois was the "most average state."
Massachusetts	Massachusetts is a state in the New England region of the northeastern United States. Most of its population of 6.4 million live in the Boston metropolitan area. The eastern half of this relatively small state is mostly urban and suburban. The west is primarily rural, also with most of its population in urban enclaves. Massachusetts is the most populous of the six New England states and ranks third in overall population density among the 50 states.
Parens patriae	Parens patriae refers to power of the state to act in behalf of the child and provide care and protection equivalent to that of a parent.
Prince	Prince from French Prince , is a general term for a monarch, for a member of a monarchs" or former monarch"s family, and is a hereditary title in some members of Europe"s highest nobility. The feminine equivalent is a Prince ss. Cicero attacks Catiline in the Senate of the Roman Republic. The Latin word prÄ«nceps , became the usual title of the informal leader of the Roman senate some centuries before the transition to empire, the Prince ps senatus.
State government	A state government is the government of a subnational entity in states with federal forms of government, which shares political power with the federal government or national government. A state government may have some level of political autonomy, or be subject to the direct control of the federal government.

Power	Power is the ability of a person to control or influence the choices of other persons. The term authority is often used for power perceived as legitimate by the social structure. Power can be seen as evil or unjust; indeed all evil and injustice committed by man against man involve power.
Government	A government is a body that has the authority to make and the power to enforce laws within a civil, corporate, religious, academic, or other organization or group.
Legislation	Legislation is law which has been promulgated by a legislature or other governing body. The term may refer to a single law, or the collective body of enacted law, while "statute" is also used to refer to a single law. Before an item of legislation becomes law it may be known as a bill, which is typically also known as "legislation" while it remains under active consideration.
Authority	In politics, authority is often used interchangeably with the term "power". However, their meanings differ: while "power" refers to the ability to achieve certain ends, "authority" refers to the legitimacy, justification and right to exercise that power. For example, whilst a mob has the power to punish a criminal, such as through lynching, only the courts have the authority to order capital punishment.
Historical	((race)) The historical definition of race was an immutable and distinct type or species, sharing distinct racial characteristics such as constitution, temperament, and mental abilities. These races were not conceived as being related with each other, but formed a hierarchy of inherent value called the Great Chain of Being with Europeans usually at the top. As time progressed, Charles Darwin"s theory of evolution was applied to races.
Cruelty	Cruelty can be described as indifference to suffering and even positive pleasure in inflicting it
Homosexuality	Homosexuality can refer to both attraction or sexual behavior between people of the same sex, or to a sexual orientation. When describing the latter, it refers to enduring sexual and romantic attraction towards those of the same sex, but not necessarily to sexual behavior.
New York	New York is a state in the Mid-Atlantic and Northeastern regions of the United States of America. With 62 counties, it is the country"s third most populous state. It is bordered by Vermont, Massachusetts, Connecticut, New Jersey, and Pennsylvania, and shares a water border with Rhode Island as well as an international border with the Canadian provinces of Quebec and Ontario. Its five largest cities are New York City, Buffalo, Rochester, Yonkers, and Syracuse.
Outdoor relief	After the passing of the Elizabethan Poor Law, outdoor relief was assistance, in the form of money, food, clothing or goods, given to alleviate poverty without the requirement that the recipient enter an institution.
Street	A street is a public thoroughfare in the built environment.

Temporary Assistance for Needy Families	Temporary Assistance for Needy Families successor to the Aid to Families with Dependent Children program, providing cash assistance to indigent American families with dependent children through the United States Department of Health and Human Services. It is the United States" federal assistance program commonly known as "welfare".
Association	Association in archaeology has more than one meaning and is confusing to the layman. Archaeology has been critiqued as a soft science with a somewhat poor standardization of terms. Associated finds or objects refers to a close relationship between two or more objects.
Federal government	A federal government is the common government of a federation. The structure of federal government s vary from institution to institution based on a broad definition of a basic federal political system, there are two or more levels of government that exist within an established territory and govern through common institutions with overlapping or shared powers as prescribed by a constitution. · Government of Australia · Government of Belgium · Government of Brazil · Government of Canada · Government of Germany · Government of India · Government of Malaysia · Government of Mexico · Government of Russia · Government of Switzerland · Government of the United States The United States is considered the first modern federation. After declaring independence from Britain, the U.S. adopted its first constitution, the Articles of Confederation in 1781.
Federation	A Federation is a type of sovereign state characterised by a union of partially self-governing states or regions united by a central government. In a Federation, the self-governing status of the component states is typically constitutionally entrenched and may not be altered by a unilateral decision of the central government. The form of government or constitutional structure found in a Federation is known as federalism
Industrial	In sociology, industrial society refers to a society with a modern societal structure. Such a structure developed in the west in the period of time following the industrial revolution. Pre-modern, or Pre-industrial society are also called agrarian societies. Industrial societies are generally mass societies.
Philadelphia	Philadelphia is the largest city in Pennsylvania and the sixth most populous city in the United States. It is the fifth largest metropolitan area by population in the United States, the nation"s fourth largest consumer media market as ranked by the Nielsen Media Research, and the 49th most populous city in the world. It is the county seat of Philadelphia County

Slavery	Slavery refers to an extreme form of stratification in which some people are owned by others.
Evidence-based practice	The term evidence-based practice refers to preferential use of mental and behavioral health interventions for which systematic empirical research has provided evidence of statistically significant effectiveness as treatments for specific problems. It is an approach which tries to specify the way in which professionals or other decision-makers should make decisions by identifying such evidence that there may be for a practice, and rating it according to how scientifically sound it may be. Its goal is to eliminate unsound or excessively risky practices in favour of those that have better outcomes.
Aid	Aid is the help, mostly economic, which may be provided to communities or countries in the event of a humanitarian crisis or to achieve a socioeconomic objective. Humanitarian aid is therefore primarily used for emergency relief, while development aid aims to create long-term sustainable economic growth. Wealthier countries typically provide aid to economically developing countries.
Aid for Dependent Children	Aid for Dependent Children was a federal assistance program, which was administered by the United States Department of Health and Human Services. Criticisms of it included there were relatively lax time limitations for participation in the program; that the program encouraged child birth to trigger or prolong benefits, and the suggestion that this had a dysgenic effect on the US population; and there were few incentives to join or rejoin the workforce, as entry level jobs could not provide the standard of living provided by it.
Dependent	The dependent variables are those that are observed to change in response to the independent variables.
Insurance	Insurance, in law and economics, is a form of risk management primarily used to hedge against the risk of a contingent loss. Insurance is defined as the equitable transfer of the risk of a loss, from one entity to another, in exchange for a premium. An insurer is a company selling the insurance. The insurance rate is a factor used to determine the amount, called the premium, to be charged for a certain amount of insurance coverage. Risk management, the practice of appraising and controlling risk, has evolved as a discrete field of study and practice.
Native Americans	Native Americans in the United States are the indigenous peoples from the regions of North America now encompassed by the continental United States, including parts of Alaska. They comprise a large number of distinct tribes, states, and ethnic groups, many of which are still enduring as political communities.
Security	Security is the condition of being protected against danger or loss.
Social	Social refers to human society or its organization. Although the term is a crucial category in social science and often used in public discourse, its meaning is at times vague, suggesting that it is a fuzzy concept. An added difficulty is that social attributes or relationships may not be directly observable and visible, and must be inferred by abstract thought.

Social Security	Social security primarily refers to social welfare service concerned with social protection, or protection against socially recognized conditions, including poverty, old age, disability, unemployment and others.
Policy	A policy is a deliberate plan of action to guide decisions and achieve rational outcomes. The term may apply to government, private sector organizations and groups, and individuals. Presidential executive orders, corporate privacy policies, and parliamentary rules of order are all examples of policy. Policy differs from rules or law. While law can compel or prohibit behaviors policy merely guides actions toward those that are most likely to achieve a desired outcome.
Adoption and Safe Families Act	The Adoption and Safe Families Act was signed into law by President Bill Clinton on November 19, 1997 after having been approved by the United States Congress earlier in the month. It was enacted in an attempt to correct problems that were inherent in the foster care system that deterred the adoption of children with special needs.
Independence	Independence is the self-government of a nation, country, or state by its residents and population, or some portion thereof, generally exercising sovereignty.
Delinquent	Delinquent means one who fails to do that which is required by law or by duty when such failure is minor in nature.
Delinquency Prevention	That which involves any nonjustice program or policy designed to prevent the occurrence of a future delinquent act is referred to as delinquency prevention.
Judicial branch	Judicial branch is the system of courts which administer justice in the name of the sovereign or state, a mechanism for the resolution of disputes. The term is also used to refer collectively to the judges, magistrates and other adjudicators who form the core of it, as well as the support personnel who keep the system running smoothly.
Justice	Justice concerns the proper ordering of things and persons within a society. As a concept it has been subject to philosophical, legal, and theological reflection and debate throughout history.
Juvenile courts	Juvenile courts are courts specifically created and given authority to try and pass judgments for crimes committed by persons who have not attained the age of majority. In most modern legal systems, crimes committed by children and minors are treated differently and differentially regarding the same crimes committed by adults.
Perspective	Perspective in theory of cognition is the choice of a context or a reference or the result of this choice from which to sense, categorize, measure or codify experience, cohesively forming a coherent belief, typically for comparing with another. One may further recognize a number of subtly distinctive meanings, close to those of paradigm, point of view, reality tunnel, umwelt, or weltanschauung.

Politician	A politician is an individual who is involved in influencing public decision making through the influence of politics or a person who influences the way a society is governed through an understanding of political power and group dynamics. This includes people who hold decision-making positions in government, and people who seek those positions, whether by means of election, coup d"état, appointment, electoral fraud, conquest, right of inheritance or other means. Politics are not limited to governance through public office.
Public	Public is about the what of belonging to the people; relating to, or affecting, a nation, state, or community; opposed to private; as, the public treasury, a road or lake. Public is also defined as the people of a nation not affiliated with the government of that nation.
Personal and cultural value	A personal and cultural value is a relative ethic value, an assumption upon which implementation can be extrapolated. A value system is a set of consistent values and measures. A principle value is a foundation upon which other values and measures of integrity are based.
Kinship	Kinship is a relationship between any entities that share a genealogical origin, through either biological, cultural, or historical descent. In anthropology the kinship system includes people related both by descent and marriage, while usage in biology includes descent and mating. Human kinship relations through marriage are commonly called "affinity" in contrast to "descent" also called "consanguinity", although the two may overlap in marriages among those of common descent. Family relations as sociocultural genealogy lead back to gods
Open adoption	A system of adoption in which the birth mother is permitted to meet and play an active role in selecting the adoptive parents and to maintain some form of contact with her child depending on the agreement reached is referred to as an open adoption.
Social network	A social network is a social structure made of nodes that are tied by one or more specific types of interdependency, such as values, visions, ideas, financial exchange, friends, kinship, dislike, conflict, trade, web links, sexual relations, disease transmission, or airline routes. The resulting structures are often very complex.
Ethnicity	Ethnicity is a population of human beings whose members identify with each other, either on the basis of a presumed common genealogy or ancestry or recognition by others as a distinct group, or by common cultural, linguistic, religious, or physical traits. The sociologist Max Weber once remarked that "The whole conception of it is so complex and so vague that it might be good to abandon it altogether."
Jim Crow laws	The Jim Crow Laws were state and local laws enacted in the Southern and border states of the United States. They mandated "separate but equal" status for black Americans. In reality, this led to treatment and accommodations that were almost always inferior to those provided to white Americans.

Child abuse	Child abuse is the physical, sexual, or emotional maltreatment or neglect of children by parents, guardians, or others. Child abuse in its various forms has numerous effects and consequences, both tangible and intangible, upon society, those mistreated, and those entrusted with the responsibility of its detection, prevention and treatment.
Race	The term race refers to the concept of dividing people into populations or groups on the basis of various sets of characteristics and beliefs about common ancestry. The most widely used human racial categories are based on visible traits especially skin color, facial features and hair texture, and self-identification.
Choice	Choice consists of the mental process of thinking involved with the process of judging the merits of multiple options and selecting one of them for action. Some simple examples include deciding whether to get up in the morning or go back to sleep, or selecting a given route for a journey. More complex examples often decisions that affect what a person thinks or their core beliefs include choosing a lifestyle, religious affiliation, or political position.
Faith-based initiatives	Faith-based initiatives is a department under the Office of the President of the United States that was established by President George W. Bush through executive order on January 29, 2001, and which represents one of the key domestic policies of Bush"s campaign promise of "compassionate conservatism." The initiative seeks to strengthen faith-based and community organizations and expand their capacity to provide federally-funded social services, with the idea being that these groups are well-situated to meet the needs of local individuals. As Texas governor Bush had used the "Charitable Choice" provisions of the 1996 welfare reform which allowed "faith-based" entities to compete for government contracts to deliver social services to support faith-based groups in Texas.
Church and state	The relationship between church and state during the medieval period went through a number of developments, roughly from the end of the Roman Empire through to the beginning of the Reformation. The events of the struggles for power between kings and popes shaped the western world. Antichristus, a woodcut by Lucas Cranach the Elder of the pope using the temporal power to grant authority to a generously contributing ruler For centuries, monarchs ruled by the idea of divine right, which said the king ruled both Crown and Church, a theory known as caesaropapism.
Cooperation	Cooperation is the practice of individuals or larger societal entities working in common with mutually agreed-upon goals and possibly methods, instead of working separately in competition, and in which the success of one is dependent and contingent upon the success of another.
Partnership	A partnership is a type of business entity in which partners share with each other the profits or losses of the business undertaking in which all have invested.
Globalization	Globalization refers to increasing global connectivity, integration and interdependence in the economic, social, technological, cultural, political, and ecological spheres. It is a unitary process inclusive of many sub-processes that are increasingly binding people and the biosphere more tightly into one global system.

Trend	A trend is something that somehow becomes popular within mainstream society over a long period of time. It is the direction of a sequence of events that has some momentum and durability.
Hague Convention	The longtime status of the Netherlands as a largely neutral nation in international conflicts and the corresponding ascendance of The Hague as a primary location for diplomatic and international conferences has led to several negotiated conventions over the years being termed the Hague Convention.
International adoption	International adoption is a type of adoption in which an individual or couple becomes the legal and permanent parents of a child born in another country. In general, prospective adoptive parents must meet the legal adoption requirements of their country of residence and those of the country in which the child was born.
New Zealand	New Zealand has a modern, prosperous, developed economy with an estimated GDP of $106 billion. The country has a high standard of living with GDP per capita estimated at $26,000. The tertiary sector is the largest sector in the economy 67.6% of GDP, followed by the secondary sector 27.8% of GDP and the primary sector 4.7% of GDP. It is heavily dependent on trade, particularly in agricultural products, and exports account for almost 28% of its output.
Exploitation	In political economy, economics, and sociology, exploitation involves a persistent social relationship in which certain persons are being mistreated or unfairly used for the benefit of others. This corresponds to one ethical conception of exploitation, that is, the treatment of human beings as mere means to an end — or as mere "objects".
Social work	Social work is a helping profession focused on social change, problem solving in human relationships and the empowerment and liberation of people to enhance well-being.
Complexity	Complexity often tends to be used to characterize something with many parts in intricate arrangement.
Training	The term training refers to the acquisition of knowledge, skills, and competencies as a result of the teaching of vocational or practical skills and knowledge that relate to specific useful competencies.
Disaster	A disaster is the impact of a natural or man-made hazards that negatively affects society or environment. They occur when hazards strike in vulnerable areas.
Mitigation and preparedness	Mitigation and preparedness are two of four phases in the discipline of dealing with and avoiding risks. It is a discipline that involves preparing, supporting, and rebuilding society when natural or human-made disasters occur.
Planning	Planning in organizations and public policy is both the organizational process of creating and maintaining a plan; and the psychological process of thinking about the activities required to create a desired future on some scale.

Detention	Temporary care of a child alleged to be delinquent who requires secure custody in physically restricting facilities pending court disposition or execution of a court order is detention.
Website	A website (or web site) is a collection of related web pages, images, videos or other digital assets that are addressed with a common domain name or IP address in an Internet Protocol-based network. A web site is hosted on at least one web server, accessible via the Internet or a private local area network. A web page is a document, typically written in plain text interspersed with formatting instructions of Hypertext Markup Language (HTML, XHTML.)
Resource	A resource is any physical or virtual entity of limited availability, or anything used to help one earn a living. In most cases, commercial or even ethic factors require resource allocation through resource management. As resource s are very useful, we attach some information value to them.
Youth	Youth is defined by as, "The time of life when one is young; especially: a: the period between childhood and maturity b: the early period of existence, growth, or development."

Chapter 2. Government Programs to Support Families and Children

Government	A government is a body that has the authority to make and the power to enforce laws within a civil, corporate, religious, academic, or other organization or group.
Family	A family consists of a domestic group of people, typically affiliated by birth or marriage, or by analogous or comparable relationships — including domestic partnership, cohabitation, adoption, surname and ownership.
Reform	A reform movement is a kind of social movement that aims to make gradual change, or change in certain aspects of society rather than rapid or fundamental changes.
Reformism	Socialist Reformism is the belief that gradual democratic changes in a society can ultimately change a society"s fundamental economic relations and political structures. This belief grew out of opposition to revolutionary socialism, which contends that revolutions are necessary to fundamentally change a society.
Temporary Assistance for Needy Families	Temporary Assistance for Needy Families successor to the Aid to Families with Dependent Children program, providing cash assistance to indigent American families with dependent children through the United States Department of Health and Human Services. It is the United States" federal assistance program commonly known as "welfare".
Welfare	Welfare is financial assistance paid by taxpayers to people who are unable to support themselves. Some welfare is general, while specific and can only be invoked under certain circumstances, such as a scholarship. Individuals may apply for welfare due to disability, lack of education or job training, a low demand for unskilled labor, substance abuse, or an unwillingness to work.
Welfare reform	Welfare reform is the name for a policy change in countries with a state-administered social welfare system to reduce dependence on welfare, as demanded by political conservatives. A movement to change the federal government"s social welfare policy which shifted responsibility to the states and cut benefits.
Assessment	Educational Assessment is the process of documenting, usually in measurable terms, knowledge, skills, attitudes and beliefs. Assessment can focus on the individual learner, the learning community (class, workshop, or other organized group of learners), the institution, or the educational system as a whole. According to the Academic Exchange Quarterly: "Studies of a theoretical or empirical nature (including case studies, portfolio studies, exploratory, or experimental work) addressing the Assessment of learner aptitude and preparation, motivation and learning styles, learning outcomes in achievement and satisfaction in different educational contexts are all welcome, as are studies addressing issues of measurable standards and benchmarks".
Credit	Credit-debt relationship is defined as 'that which is owed by one entity to another.' An entity may be an individual, company, government or any other type of institution or organization. Credit and debt represent flip sides of the same coin. Credit is that which is provided, debt that which is owed

Earned Income Tax Credit	The United States federal Earned Income Tax Credit is a refundable tax credit. It is one of the largest anti-poverty tools in the United States and enjoys broad bipartisan support. Grandparents, aunts, uncles, and siblings can also claim a child as their qualifying child provided they have shared residence with the child for more than half the tax year.
Family income	Family income is generally considered a primary measure of a nation"s financial prosperity.
Income	Income, generally defined, is the money that is received as a result of the normal business activities of an individual or a business.
Income Tax	An income tax is a tax levied on the financial income of persons, corporations, or other legal entities. Various income tax systems exist, with varying degrees of tax incidence. It can be progressive, proportional, or regressive. Personal income tax is often collected on a pay-as-you-earn basis, with small corrections made soon after the end of the tax year.
Personal Responsibility and Work Opportunity Reconciliation Act	The Personal Responsibility and Work Opportunity Reconciliation Act of 1996 is a United States federal law considered to be a fundamental shift in both the method and goal of federal cash assistance to the poor.
Poverty	Poverty may be seen as the collective condition of poor people, or of poor groups, and in this sense entire nation-states are sometimes regarded as poor. Although the most severe poverty is in the developing world, there is evidence of poverty in every region.
Poverty line	The poverty threshold, or poverty line, is the level of income below which one cannot afford to purchase all the resources one requires to live. Thus, by definition, nobody lives below the poverty line.
Security	Security is the condition of being protected against danger or loss.
Statistics	Statistics is a mathematical science pertaining to the collection, analysis, interpretation, and presentation of data. It is applicable to a wide variety of academic disciplines, from the physical and social sciences to the humanities; it is also used and misused for making informed decisions in all areas of business and government.
African Americans	African Americans are citizens or residents of the United States whose ancestors, usually in predominant part, were indigenous to Sub-Saharan Africa. Most are the descendants of captive Africans who were enslaved within the boundaries of the present United States.
Consumer	A consumer is an individual that purchases and use goods and services generated within the economy. It is often claimed that, in free market or capitalist economies, a consumer dictates what goods are produced and are generally considered the center of economic activity.

Consumer Price Index	A consumer price index is an index number measuring the average price of consumer goods and services purchased by households. It is one of several price indices calculated by national statistical agencies. The consumer price index is one of the most closely watched national economic statistics.
Wage	A wage is a compensation workers receive in exchange for their labor.
White people	White people is a term which is usually used to refer to human beings characterized, at least in part, by the light pigmentation of their skin. It often refers narrowly to people claiming ancestry exclusively from Europe. A broadly corresponding concept was the Caucasian race.
Adoption	Adoption is the legal act of permanently placing a child with a parent or parents other than the birth mother or father. An adoption order has the effect of severing the parental responsibilities and rights of the birth parents and transferring those responsibilities and rights onto the adoptive parents.
Child	A child is a boy or girl who has not reached puberty, but also refers to offspring of any age.
Rates	Rates is a Portuguese parish and town located in the municipality of Póvoa de Varzim. In the census of 2001, it had a population of 2,539 inhabitants and a total area of 13.88 square kilometres. Rates is a historic small town that developed around the Monastery of Rates, established by Henry of Burgundy in 1100 AD on the site of an older temple.
Cultural diversity	Cultural diversity is the variety of human societies or cultures in a specific region, or in the world as a whole.
Education	Education encompasses teaching and learning specific skills, and also something less tangible but more profound: the imparting of knowledge, positive judgement and well-developed wisdom. Education has as one of its fundamental aspects the imparting of culture from generation to generation.
Immigration	Although human migration has existed for hundreds of thousands of years, immigration in the modern sense refers to movement of people from one nation-state to another, where they are not citizens.
Marriage	A marriage is an interpersonal relationship with governmental, social, or religious recognition, usually intimate and sexual, and often created as a contract. The most frequently occurring form of marriage unites a man and a woman as husband and wife. Other forms of marriage also exist; for example, polygamy, in which a person takes more than one spouse, is common in many societies
Minimum wage	A minimum wage is the lowest hourly, daily, or monthly wage that employers may legally pay to employees or workers. First enacted in Australia and New Zealand in the late nineteenth century,[1] minimum wage laws are now enforced in more than 90% of all countries.[2]

Mother	A mother is a biological and/or social female parent of an offspring. In the case of a mammal such as a human, the biological mother gestates a fertilized ovum, which is called first an embryo, and then a fetus. This gestation occurs in the mother"s uterus from conception until the fetus is sufficiently developed to be born. The mother then goes into labor and gives birth. Once the child is born, the mother produces milk in a process called lactation to feed the child; often the mother"s breast milk is the child"s sole nourishment for the first year or more of the child"s life.
Single-parent	A Single-parent is a parent who cares for children without the assistance of another person in the home. The legal definition of "single parenthood" may vary according to the local laws of different nations or regions.
Teenage pregnancy	Teenage pregnancy is defined as an underaged girl becoming pregnant with a baby. While women technically stay in their "teens" until the age of 20, the term is restricted to those under the age threshold of legal adulthood, which is 18 in most of the United States, and 16 in much of the rest of the world.
Urban Institute	The Urban Institute is a Washington, D.C. based nonpartisan think tank that collects data, conducts policy research, evaluates social programs, educates the public on key domestic issues, and provides advice and technical assistance to developing governments abroad. It was established the Lyndon B. Johnson administration to study the nation's urban problems and evaluate the Great Society initiatives.
Working poor	Working poor is a term used to describe individuals and families who maintain regular employment but remain in relative poverty due to low levels of pay and dependent expenses.
Assimilation	A minority group's internalization of the values and norms of the dominant culture is referred to as assimilation.
Child advocacy	Child advocacy refers to a range of individuals, professionals and advocacy organizations who promote the optimal development of children. An individual or organization engaging in advocacy typically seeks to protect children"s rights which may be abridged or abused in a number of areas. Rights can be divided into two categories: negative (rights to be free from) and positive (rights to).
Pregnancy	Pregnancy is the carrying of one or more offspring, known as a fetus or embryo, inside the body of a female mammal such as a human, between conception and birth. In many societies" medical and legal definitions, human pregnancy is somewhat arbitrarily divided into three trimester periods, as a means to simplify reference to the different stages of prenatal development.
Experience	Experience as a general concept comprises knowledge of or skill in or observation of some thing or some event gained through involvement in or exposure to that thing or event. The history of the word experience aligns it closely with the concept of experiment.
Foreign worker	A foreign worker is a person who works in a country other than the one of which he or she is a citizen.

Parenting	Parenting is the process of raizing and educating a child from birth until adulthood.
Single parent	A single parent is a parent who cares for one or more children without the assistance of another parent in the home. The legal definition may vary according to the local laws of different nations or regions.
Structure	Structure is a fundamental and sometimes intangible notion covering the recognition, observation, nature, and stability of patterns and relationships of entities. From a child"s verbal description of a snowflake, to the detailed scientific analysis of the properties of magnetic fields, the concept of structure is an essential foundation of nearly every mode of inquiry and discovery in science, philosophy, and art. A structure defines what a system is made of.
Outdoor relief	After the passing of the Elizabethan Poor Law, outdoor relief was assistance, in the form of money, food, clothing or goods, given to alleviate poverty without the requirement that the recipient enter an institution.
Pension	In general, a Pension is an arrangement to provide people with an income when they are no longer earning a regular income from employment. Pension s should not be confused with severance packages; the former is paid in regular installments, while the latter is paid in one lump sum. The terms retirement plan or superannuation refer to a Pension granted upon retirement .
Public	Public is about the what of belonging to the people; relating to, or affecting, a nation, state, or community; opposed to private; as, the public treasury, a road or lake. Public is also defined as the people of a nation not affiliated with the government of that nation.
Aid	Aid is the help, mostly economic, which may be provided to communities or countries in the event of a humanitarian crisis or to achieve a socioeconomic objective. Humanitarian aid is therefore primarily used for emergency relief, while development aid aims to create long-term sustainable economic growth. Wealthier countries typically provide aid to economically developing countries.
Aid for Dependent Children	Aid for Dependent Children was a federal assistance program, which was administered by the United States Department of Health and Human Services. Criticisms of it included there were relatively lax time limitations for participation in the program; that the program encouraged child birth to trigger or prolong benefits, and the suggestion that this had a dysgenic effect on the US population; and there were few incentives to join or rejoin the workforce, as entry level jobs could not provide the standard of living provided by it.
Dependent	The dependent variables are those that are observed to change in response to the independent variables.

Family Support Act	The Family Support Act is a Uniform Act that has been adopted by every U.S. State, in order to address the widespread problem of non-payment of child support obligations, and to limit the jurisdiction that could properly establish and modify child support orders. The Act was drafted by the National Conference of Commissioners on Uniform State Laws in 1992, and revised in 1996, and again in 2001. In 1996, the U.S. Congress passed the Personal Responsibility and Work Opportunity Act, which required the adoption of the UIFSA in all states by January 1, 1998, or face loss of federal funding for child support enforcement.
Health	Health is the level of functional and/or metabolic efficiency of an organism at both the micro and macro level. In the medical field, health is commonly defined as an organism"s ability to efficiently respond to challenges and effectively restore and sustain a "state of balance," known as homeostasis.
Human	A Human is a member of a species of bipedal primates in the family Hominidae . DNA and fossil evidence indicates that modern Human s originated in east Africa about 200,000 years ago. When compared to other animals and primates, Human s have a highly developed brain, capable of abstract reasoning, language, introspection and problem solving.
Safety	Safety is the state of being "safe", the condition of being protected against physical, social, spiritual, financial, political, emotional, occupational, psychological, educational or other types or consequences of failure, damage, error, accidents, harm or any other event which could be considered non-desirable.
Participation	Participation in social science is an umbrella term including different means for the public to directly participate in political, economic, management or other social decisions. Ideally, each actor would have a say in decisions directly proportional to the degree that particular decision affects him or her.
Food Stamp	The US Food Stamp Program is a federal assistance program that provides food to low and no income people living in the United States. Benefits are distributed by the individual states, but the program is administered through the U.S. Department of Agriculture. Most food stamp benefits are now distributed using cards but for most of its history the program had actually used paper denominational stamps/coupons in 1"s, 5"s, and 10"s.
Health Insurance	Health insurance is a type of insurance whereby the insurer pays the medical costs of the insured if the insured becomes sick due to covered causes, or due to accidents. The insurer may be a private organization or a government agency. Market-based health care systems such as that in the United States rely primarily on private health insurance.
Medicaid	Medicaid is the United States health insurance program for individuals and families with low incomes and resources. It is jointly funded by the states and federal government, and is managed by the states. Among the groups of people served by Medicaid are eligible low-income parents, children, seniors, and people with disabilities.

Budget	Budget generally refers to a list of all planned expenses and revenues.
Center on Budget and Policy Priorities	The Center on Budget and Policy Priorities is a non-profit think tank which describes itself as a "policy organization ... working at the federal and state levels on fiscal policy and public programs that affect low- and moderate-income families and individuals."
Infant	In basic English usage, an infant is defined as a human child at the youngest stage of life, specifically before they can walk and generally before the age of one.
Policy	A policy is a deliberate plan of action to guide decisions and achieve rational outcomes. The term may apply to government, private sector organizations and groups, and individuals. Presidential executive orders, corporate privacy policies, and parliamentary rules of order are all examples of policy. Policy differs from rules or law. While law can compel or prohibit behaviors policy merely guides actions toward those that are most likely to achieve a desired outcome.
Women	A woman is a female human. The term woman irregular plural: women usually is used for an adult, with the term girl being the usual term for a female child or adolescent. However, the term woman is also sometimes used to identify a female human, regardless of age, as in phrases such as "Women"s rights".
Brookings Institution	The Brookings Institution is a nonprofit public policy organization based in Washington, D.C. One of Washington"s oldest think tanks, it conducts research and education in the social sciences, primarily in economics, metropolitan policy, governance, foreign policy, and global economy and development. Their stated mission is to "provide innovative and practical recommendations that advance three broad goals: strengthen American democracy; foster the economic and social welfare, security and opportunity of all Americans and; secure a more open, safe, prosperous and cooperative international system."
Child Support	Child support is the ongoing obligation for a periodic payment made by a non-custodial parent to a custodial parent, caregiver or guardian, for the care and support of children of a relationship or marriage that has been terminated. Child support is based on the policy that parents are obligated to pay for the support of their children, even when the children are not living with both biological parents.
Coming into force	Coming into force refers to the date and process by which legislation, or part of legislation, comes to have legal force and effect.
Social	Social refers to human society or its organization. Although the term is a crucial category in social science and often used in public discourse, its meaning is at times vague, suggesting that it is a fuzzy concept. An added difficulty is that social attributes or relationships may not be directly observable and visible, and must be inferred by abstract thought.

Social Security	Social security primarily refers to social welfare service concerned with social protection, or protection against socially recognized conditions, including poverty, old age, disability, unemployment and others.
Social insurance	Social insurance refers to social programs offering benefits to broad categories of people, such as the elderly or injured workers, who presumably were working and paying for the insurance before becoming eligible for it.
Disability	Disability is lack of ability relative to a personal or group standard or spectrum. Disability may involve physical impairment, sensory impairment, cognitive or intellectual impairment, mental disorder also known as psychiatric disability, or various types of chronic disease. A disability may occur during a person"s lifetime or may be present from birth.
Old age	Old age consists of ages nearing or surpassing the average life span of human beings, and thus the end of the human life cycle. Some believe there to be prejudice against older people in Western cultures, which is one form of ageism.
Survivor	Survivor is a popular reality television game show format produced in many countries throughout the world. In the show, contestants are isolated in the wilderness and compete for cash and other prizes. The show uses a progressive elimination, allowing the contestants to vote off a tribe member, until only one final contestant remains and wins the title of "Sole Survivor". The format for Survivor was created in 1992 by Charlie Parsons, and the first production of it was the Swedish show Expedition: Robinson in 1997.
Supplemental Security Income	Supplemental Security Income is a monthly stipend provided to aged, blind, or disabled persons based on need, paid by the United States Government. The program is administered by the Social Security Administration. The program was created to replace various state-administered programs which served the same purpose, as a way to standardize in the level of benefits through the addition of Title XVI of the Social Security Act.
Unemployment	Unemployment is the condition of willing workers lacking jobs or "gainful employment". A key measure is the unemployment rate, which is the number of unemployed workers divided by the total civilian labor force.
Unemployment insurance	Unemployment insurance is payments made by governments to unemployed people. It may be based on a compulsory para-governmental insurance system. It is generally given only to those registering as unemployed, and often on conditions ensuring that they seek work and do not currently have a job.
Construction	In the fields of architecture and civil engineering, construction is a process that consists of the building or assembling of infrastructure. Far from being a single activity, large scale construction is a feat of multitasking. Normally the job is managed by the project manager and supervised by the construction manager, design engineer, construction engineer or project architect.

Day care	Day care is a term used to describe the care of a child during the day by a person other than the child"s parents or legal guardians, typically someone outside the child"s immediate family.
Day	A Day (symbol d) is a unit of time equivalent to approximately 24 hours. It is not an SI unit but it is accepted for use with SI. The SI unit of time is the second. The word Day can also refer to the (roughly) half of the Day that is not night, also known as " Day time".
Lanham Act	The Lanham Act is a piece of legislation that contains the federal statutes of trademark law in the United States.
Block Grant	A block grant is a large sum of money granted by the national government to a regional government with only general provisions as to the way it is to be spent. An advantage of it is that it allows regional governments to experiment with different ways of spending money with the same goal in mind, though it is very difficult to compare the results of such spending and reach a conclusion.
Household and Dependent Care Credit	The Household and Dependent Care Credit is a nonrefundable tax credit available to United States taxpayers. Taxpayers that care for a qualifying individual are eligible. The purpose of the credit is to allow the taxpayer (or their spouse, if married) to be gainfully employed.
Family and Medical Leave Act	The Family and Medical Leave Act is a United States labor law allowing an employee to take unpaid leave due to a serious health condition that makes the employee unable to perform his job or to care for a sick family member or to care for a new son or daughter. It was one of the first major bills signed by President Bill Clinton in his first term, fulfilling a campaign promise.
Head Start	Head Start is a program of the United States Department of Health and Human Services that focuses on assisting children from low-income families. Created in 1965, Head Start is the longest-running national school readiness program in the United States. It provides comprehensive education, health, nutrition, and parent involvement services to low-income children and their families.
Legislation	Legislation is law which has been promulgated by a legislature or other governing body. The term may refer to a single law, or the collective body of enacted law, while "statute" is also used to refer to a single law. Before an item of legislation becomes law it may be known as a bill, which is typically also known as "legislation" while it remains under active consideration.
Workforce	The workforce is the labor pool in employment. It is generally used to describe those working for a single company or industry. The term generally excludes the employers or management, and implies those involved in manual labor. It may also mean all those that are available for work.
Regulation	Regulation can be considered as legal restrictions promulgated by government authority.
Youth	Youth is defined by as, "The time of life when one is young; especially: a: the period between childhood and maturity b: the early period of existence, growth, or development."

Human Development	Human development is the scientific study of progressive psychological changes that occur in human beings as they age. Originally concerned with infants and children, and later other periods of great change such as adolescence and aging, it now encompasses the entire life span.
Human Development report	The Human Development Report is an annual milestone publication by the United Nations Development Program. Its goal was to place people at the centre of the development process in terms of economic debate, policy and advocacy. Each Report has its own focus drawn from contemporary debate.
Violence	*Violence* is the exertion of force with the intent to injure (psychologically or physically) or kill. *Violence* is also used more broadly and metaphorically to describe the destructive action of natural phenomena like storms and earthquakes. Variant uses of the term refer to the destruction of non-living objects
Quality of life	The quality of life of a population is an important concern in economics and political science. It is measured by many social and economic factors. A large part is standard of living, the amount of money and access to goods and services that a person has; these numbers are fairly easily measured.
Adolescence	Adolescence (lat adolescere, (to grow) is a transitional stage of physical and mental human development that occurs between childhood and adulthood. This transition involves biological (i.e. pubertal), social, and psychological changes, though the biological or physiological ones are the easiest to measure objectively. Historically, puberty has been heavily associated with teenagers and the onset of adolescent development.[1][2] In recent years, however, the start of puberty has had somewhat of an increase in preAdolescence (particularly females), and Adolescence has had an occasional extension beyond the teenage years (typically males).
Birth rate	Crude Birth rate is the nativity or childbirths per 1,000 people per year. It can be represented by number of childbirths in that year, and p is the current population. This figure is combined with the crude death rate to produce the rate of natural population growth (natural in that it does not take into account net migration.)
Crude Birth rate	The number of live births per 1000 people in a population in a given year is a crude birth rate.
Minor	In law, the term minor is used to refer to a person who is under the age in which one legally assumes adulthood and is legally granted rights afforded to adults in society. Depending on the jurisdiction and application, this age may vary, but is usually marked at either 18 or 21. Specifically, the status of "minor" is defined by the age of majority[
Mathematics	Mathematics is the body of knowledge centered on such concepts as quantity, structure, space, and change, and also the academic discipline that studies them. Benjamin Peirce called it "the science that draws necessary conclusions".

Overweight	The term overweight is generally used to indicate that a human has more body fat than is considered useful for the optimal functioning of the body. Being overweight is a fairly common condition for many people, especially those in developed nations where food supplies are plentiful and lifestyles often do not involve a lot of activities that generate caloric expenditure.
Delinquent	Delinquent means one who fails to do that which is required by law or by duty when such failure is minor in nature.
Income support	Income Support is an income-related means-tested benefit in the United Kingdom for people who are on a low income. Claimants of Income Support may be entitled to certain other benefits, for example, Housing Benefit, Council Tax Benefit and help with health costs. A person with savings over Â£16,000 cannot get Income Support and savings over Â£6,000 affect how much Income Support can be received.
School	A school is an institution where students learn while under the supervision of teachers. In most systems of formal education, students progress through a series of schools: primary school, secondary school, and possibly a university or vocational school. A school may also be dedicated to one particular field, such as a school of economics or a school of dance.
Employment	Employment is a contract between two parties, one being the employer and the other being the employee. An employee may be defined as: "A person in the service of another under any contract of hire, express or implied, oral or written, where the employer has the power or right to control and direct the employee in the material details of how the work is to be performed."
Population	A population is the collection of people or organisms of a particular species living in a given geographic area or space, usually measured by a census.
Addiction	A pattern of behavior characterized by an overwhelming involvement with using a drug and securing its supply is defined as an addiction.
Alcohol abuse	Alcohol abuse, as described in the DSM-IV, is a psychiatric diagnosis describing the use of alcoholic beverages despite negative consequences.
Child Protective Services	Child Protective Services is the name of a governmental agency in many states in the United States that responds to allegations of child abuse or neglect.
Domestic violence	Domestic violence occurs when a family member, partner or ex-partner attempts to physically or psychologically dominate another. Domestic violence often refers to violence between spouses, or spousal abuse but can also include cohabitants and non-married intimate partners. Domestic violence occurs in all cultures; people of all races, ethnicities, religions, sexes and classes can be perpetrators of domestic violence. Domestic violence is perpetrated by both men and women.

Drug	A drug is any chemical or biological substance, synthetic or non-synthetic, that when taken into the organism"s body, will in some way alter the functions of that organism. This broad definition can be taken to include such substances as food.
Drug abuse	Drug abuse has a wide range of definitions related to taking a psychoactive drug or performance enhancing drug for a non-therapeutic or non-medical effect.. Public health practitioners have attempted to look at drug abuse from a broader perspective than the individual, emphasising the role of society, culture and availability.
Foster care	Foster care is a system by which a certified, stand-in "parent" cares for minor children or young peoples who have been removed from their birth parents or other custodial adults by state authority. Responsibility for the young person is assumed by the relevant governmental authority and a placement with another family found. There can be voluntary placements by a parent of a child into foster care.
Internet	The Internet is a global system of interconnected computer networks that interchange data by packet switching using the standardized Internet Protocol Suite. It is a "network of networks" that consists of millions of private and public, academic, business, and government networks of local to global scope that are linked by copper wires, fiber-optic cables, wireless connections, and other technologies. The Internet carries various information resources and services, such as electronic mail, online chat, file transfer and file sharing, online gaming, and the inter-linked hypertext documents and other resources of the World Wide Web.
Trend	A trend is something that somehow becomes popular within mainstream society over a long period of time. It is the direction of a sequence of events that has some momentum and durability.
Website	A website (or web site) is a collection of related web pages, images, videos or other digital assets that are addressed with a common domain name or IP address in an Internet Protocol-based network. A web site is hosted on at least one web server, accessible via the Internet or a private local area network. A web page is a document, typically written in plain text interspersed with formatting instructions of Hypertext Markup Language (HTML, XHTML.)
Association	Association in archaeology has more than one meaning and is confusing to the layman. Archaeology has been critiqued as a soft science with a somewhat poor standardization of terms. Associated finds or objects refers to a close relationship between two or more objects.
Research	Research is defined as human activity based on intellectual application in the investigation of matter. The primary aim for applied research is discovering, interpreting, and the development of methods and systems for the advancement of human knowledge on a wide variety of scientific matters of our world and the universe. Research can use the scientific method, but need not do so.

Family	A family consists of a domestic group of people, typically affiliated by birth or marriage, or by analogous or comparable relationships — including domestic partnership, cohabitation, adoption, surname and ownership.
Community	A community is a social group of organisms sharing an environment, normally with shared interests. In human communities, intent, belief, resources, preferences, needs, risks and a number of other conditions may be present and common, affecting the identity of the participants and their degree of cohesiveness.
Community service	Community service refers to service that a person performs for the benefit of his or her local community. People become involved in community service for a range of reasons, for some, it is an altruistic act, for others it is a punishment.
Assessment	Educational Assessment is the process of documenting, usually in measurable terms, knowledge, skills, attitudes and beliefs. Assessment can focus on the individual learner, the learning community (class, workshop, or other organized group of learners), the institution, or the educational system as a whole. According to the Academic Exchange Quarterly: "Studies of a theoretical or empirical nature (including case studies, portfolio studies, exploratory, or experimental work) addressing the Assessment of learner aptitude and preparation, motivation and learning styles, learning outcomes in achievement and satisfaction in different educational contexts are all welcome, as are studies addressing issues of measurable standards and benchmarks".
Family Preservation	Family preservation was the movement to help keep children at home with their families rather than in foster homes or institutions. This movement was a reaction to the earlier policy of family breakup, which pulled children out of unfit homes. Extreme poverty alone was seen as a justified reason to remove children.
Internet	The Internet is a global system of interconnected computer networks that interchange data by packet switching using the standardized Internet Protocol Suite. It is a "network of networks" that consists of millions of private and public, academic, business, and government networks of local to global scope that are linked by copper wires, fiber-optic cables, wireless connections, and other technologies. The Internet carries various information resources and services, such as electronic mail, online chat, file transfer and file sharing, online gaming, and the inter-linked hypertext documents and other resources of the World Wide Web.
Need	A Need is something that is necessary for humans to live a healthy life. Need s are distinguished from wants because a deficiency would cause a clear negative outcome, such as dysfunction or death. Need s can be objective and physical, such as food and water, or they can be subjective and psychological, such as the Need for self-esteem.
Abuse	Abuse refers to the use or treatment of something that is seen as harmful. The term can be used for anything ranging from the misuse of a piece of equipment to the severe maltreatment of a person.
Child	A child is a boy or girl who has not reached puberty, but also refers to offspring of any age.

Child Abuse	Child abuse is the physical, sexual, or emotional maltreatment or neglect of children by parents, guardians, or others. Child abuse in its various forms has numerous effects and consequences, both tangible and intangible, upon society, those mistreated, and those entrusted with the responsibility of its detection, prevention and treatment.
Cultural diversity	Cultural diversity is the variety of human societies or cultures in a specific region, or in the world as a whole.
Father	The father is defined as the male parent of an offspring. The adjective "paternal" refers to father, parallel to "maternal" for mother. According to the anthropologist Maurice Godelier, the parental role assumed by human males is a critical difference between human society and that of humans" closest biological relatives - chimpanzees and bonobos - who appear to be unaware of their "father" connection.
Marriage	A marriage is an interpersonal relationship with governmental, social, or religious recognition, usually intimate and sexual, and often created as a contract. The most frequently occurring form of marriage unites a man and a woman as husband and wife. Other forms of marriage also exist; for example, polygamy, in which a person takes more than one spouse, is common in many societies
Mother	A mother is a biological and/or social female parent of an offspring. In the case of a mammal such as a human, the biological mother gestates a fertilized ovum, which is called first an embryo, and then a fetus. This gestation occurs in the mother"s uterus from conception until the fetus is sufficiently developed to be born. The mother then goes into labor and gives birth. Once the child is born, the mother produces milk in a process called lactation to feed the child; often the mother"s breast milk is the child"s sole nourishment for the first year or more of the child"s life.
Single-parent	A Single-parent is a parent who cares for children without the assistance of another person in the home. The legal definition of "single parenthood" may vary according to the local laws of different nations or regions.
Adoption	Adoption is the legal act of permanently placing a child with a parent or parents other than the birth mother or father. An adoption order has the effect of severing the parental responsibilities and rights of the birth parents and transferring those responsibilities and rights onto the adoptive parents.
Experience	Experience as a general concept comprises knowledge of or skill in or observation of some thing or some event gained through involvement in or exposure to that thing or event. The history of the word experience aligns it closely with the concept of experiment.
Single parent	A single parent is a parent who cares for one or more children without the assistance of another parent in the home. The legal definition may vary according to the local laws of different nations or regions.

Structure	Structure is a fundamental and sometimes intangible notion covering the recognition, observation, nature, and stability of patterns and relationships of entities. From a child"s verbal description of a snowflake, to the detailed scientific analysis of the properties of magnetic fields, the concept of structure is an essential foundation of nearly every mode of inquiry and discovery in science, philosophy, and art. A structure defines what a system is made of.
Family values	Family values is a political and social concept or term that has been used in various nations across the world to describe a set of varied and often ambiguous moral beliefs in society specifically in response to the perception by social or religious conservatives of declining morality within that nation itself. It"s concept is rooted in each individual culture thus making the values different for different societies.
Gay	Gay usually describes a person"s sexual orientation, being the standard term for homosexual. Gay sometimes also refers to commonalities shared by homosexual people, as in "gay history", the ideological concept of a hypothetical gay culture, as in "gay music." The word gay is sometimes used to refer to same-sex relationships.
LGBT parenting	LGBT parenting refers to lesbian, gay, bisexual, and transgendered people that are parents. Common methods of LGBT parenting are adoption, donor insemination, foster parenting, and surrogacy, as well as parenting by a mother or father who was previously in a heterosexual relationship.
Lesbian	A lesbian is a woman who is romantically and sexually attracted only to other women. Some women in same-sex relationships do not identify as lesbian, but as bisexual, queer, or another label. As with any interpersonal activity, sexual expression depends on the context of the relationship.
African Americans	African Americans are citizens or residents of the United States whose ancestors, usually in predominant part, were indigenous to Sub-Saharan Africa. Most are the descendants of captive Africans who were enslaved within the boundaries of the present United States.
Teenage pregnancy	Teenage pregnancy is defined as an underaged girl becoming pregnant with a baby. While women technically stay in their "teens" until the age of 20, the term is restricted to those under the age threshold of legal adulthood, which is 18 in most of the United States, and 16 in much of the rest of the world.
Pregnancy	Pregnancy is the carrying of one or more offspring, known as a fetus or embryo, inside the body of a female mammal such as a human, between conception and birth. In many societies" medical and legal definitions, human pregnancy is somewhat arbitrarily divided into three trimester periods, as a means to simplify reference to the different stages of prenatal development.

Statistics	Statistics is a mathematical science pertaining to the collection, analysis, interpretation, and presentation of data. It is applicable to a wide variety of academic disciplines, from the physical and social sciences to the humanities; it is also used and misused for making informed decisions in all areas of business and government.
Government	A government is a body that has the authority to make and the power to enforce laws within a civil, corporate, religious, academic, or other organization or group.
Personal Responsibility and Work Opportunity Reconciliation Act	The Personal Responsibility and Work Opportunity Reconciliation Act of 1996 is a United States federal law considered to be a fundamental shift in both the method and goal of federal cash assistance to the poor.
Reform	A reform movement is a kind of social movement that aims to make gradual change, or change in certain aspects of society rather than rapid or fundamental changes.
Reformism	Socialist Reformism is the belief that gradual democratic changes in a society can ultimately change a society"s fundamental economic relations and political structures. This belief grew out of opposition to revolutionary socialism, which contends that revolutions are necessary to fundamentally change a society.
State government	A state government is the government of a subnational entity in states with federal forms of government, which shares political power with the federal government or national government. A state government may have some level of political autonomy, or be subject to the direct control of the federal government.
Parenting	Parenting is the process of raizing and educating a child from birth until adulthood.
Risk	Risk is a concept that denotes the precise probability of specific eventualities. Technically, the notion of Risk is independent from the notion of value and, as such, eventualities may have both beneficial and adverse consequences. However, in general usage the convention is to focus only on potential negative impact to some characteristic of value that may arise from a future event.
Welfare	Welfare is financial assistance paid by taxpayers to people who are unable to support themselves. Some welfare is general, while specific and can only be invoked under certain circumstances, such as a scholarship. Individuals may apply for welfare due to disability, lack of education or job training, a low demand for unskilled labor, substance abuse, or an unwillingness to work.
Welfare reform	Welfare reform is the name for a policy change in countries with a state-administered social welfare system to reduce dependence on welfare, as demanded by political conservatives. A movement to change the federal government"s social welfare policy which shifted responsibility to the states and cut benefits.

Cultural Competence	Cultural competence refers to an ability to interact effectively with people of different cultures.
Immigration	Although human migration has existed for hundreds of thousands of years, immigration in the modern sense refers to movement of people from one nation-state to another, where they are not citizens.
Social	Social refers to human society or its organization. Although the term is a crucial category in social science and often used in public discourse, its meaning is at times vague, suggesting that it is a fuzzy concept. An added difficulty is that social attributes or relationships may not be directly observable and visible, and must be inferred by abstract thought.
Social Work	Social work is a helping profession focused on social change, problem solving in human relationships and the empowerment and liberation of people to enhance well-being.
Urban Institute	The Urban Institute is a Washington, D.C. based nonpartisan think tank that collects data, conducts policy research, evaluates social programs, educates the public on key domestic issues, and provides advice and technical assistance to developing governments abroad. It was established the Lyndon B. Johnson administration to study the nation's urban problems and evaluate the Great Society initiatives.
Assimilation	A minority group's internalization of the values and norms of the dominant culture is referred to as assimilation.
Quality of life	The quality of life of a population is an important concern in economics and political science. It is measured by many social and economic factors. A large part is standard of living, the amount of money and access to goods and services that a person has; these numbers are fairly easily measured.
Extended family	Extended family refers to a family group consisting of more than two generations of the same kinship line living either within the same household or, more usually in the west, very close to one another.
Hurricane	A hurricane is one of many meteorological terms for a storm system characterized by a low pressure center and thunderstorms that produces strong wind and flooding rain. It feeds on the heat released when moist air rises and the water vapor it contains condenses.
Hurricane Katrina	Hurricane Katrina was the costliest and one of the five deadliest hurricanes in the history of the United States. It was the sixth-strongest Atlantic hurricane ever recorded and the third-strongest hurricane on record that made landfall in the United States. Katrina formed on August 23 during the 2005 Atlantic hurricane season and caused devastation along much of the north-central Gulf Coast. The most severe loss of life and property damage occurred in New Orleans, Louisiana, which flooded as the levee system catastrophically failed, in many cases hours after the storm had moved inland.

Kinship	Kinship is a relationship between any entities that share a genealogical origin, through either biological, cultural, or historical descent. In anthropology the kinship system includes people related both by descent and marriage, while usage in biology includes descent and mating. Human kinship relations through marriage are commonly called "affinity" in contrast to "descent" also called "consanguinity", although the two may overlap in marriages among those of common descent. Family relations as sociocultural genealogy lead back to gods
Role	A role or a social role is a set of connected behaviors, rights and obligations as conceptualized by actors in a social situation. It is an expected behavior in a given individual social status and social position. It is vital to both functionalist and interactionist understandings of society.
Jim Crow laws	The Jim Crow Laws were state and local laws enacted in the Southern and border states of the United States. They mandated "separate but equal" status for black Americans. In reality, this led to treatment and accommodations that were almost always inferior to those provided to white Americans.
Slavery	Slavery refers to an extreme form of stratification in which some people are owned by others.
Family of Love	The Family of Love were a mystic religious sect known as the Familia Caritatis, founded by Hendrik Niclaes.
Godparent	A godparent, in many denominations of Christianity, is someone who sponsors a child"s baptism. Judaism has this equivalent in the circumcision ceremony. A male godparent is a godfather and a female godparent is a godmother.
Social role	A social role is a set of connected behaviors, rights and obligations as conceptualized by actors in a social situation. It is mostly defined as an expected behavior in a given individual social status and social position.
Infant	In basic English usage, an infant is defined as a human child at the youngest stage of life, specifically before they can walk and generally before the age of one.
Infant mortality	Infant mortality is the death of infants in the first year of life. The most common causes of infant mortality worldwide has traditionally been dehydration from diarrhea and pneumonia.
Infant mortality rate	Infant mortality rate is the number of newborns dying under a year of age divided by the number of live births during the year. Infant mortality rate is commonly included as a part of standard of living evaluations in economics.
Native Americans	Native Americans in the United States are the indigenous peoples from the regions of North America now encompassed by the continental United States, including parts of Alaska. They comprise a large number of distinct tribes, states, and ethnic groups, many of which are still enduring as political communities.

Register	Register is a term that refers to pictographic representation of a scene, and its separation from an adjoining scene by putting the scene in regestered sections. This term can be applied in sculpture, or ancient artwork, or languages. Scenes are typically separated by lines, with each straight line separating the scenes into Block registers.
United States	The United States is a constitutional federal republic comprising fifty states and a federal district. The country is situated mostly in central North America, where its forty-eight contiguous states and Washington, D.C., the capital district, lie between the Pacific and Atlantic Oceans, bordered by Canada to the north and Mexico to the south.
Women	A woman is a female human. The term woman irregular plural: women usually is used for an adult, with the term girl being the usual term for a female child or adolescent. However, the term woman is also sometimes used to identify a female human, regardless of age, as in phrases such as "Women"s rights".
Force	In physics, a force is action which can cause an object with mass to accelerate. Force has both magnitude and direction, making it a vector quantity. According to Newton"s second law, an object with constant mass will accelerate in proportion to the net force acting upon it and in inverse proportion to its mass.
Labor	In economics, labor is a measure of the work done by human beings. It is conventionally contrasted with such other factors of production as land and capital. There are theories which have created a concept called human capital, although there are also counter posing macro-economic system theories that think human capital is a contradiction in terms.
Labor force	In economics the people in the labor force are the suppliers of labor. The fraction of the labor force that is seeking work but cannot find it determines the unemployment rate. The labor force participation rate is the ratio between the labor force and the overall size of their cohort.
Rates	Rates is a Portuguese parish and town located in the municipality of Póvoa de Varzim. In the census of 2001, it had a population of 2,539 inhabitants and a total area of 13.88 square kilometres. Rates is a historic small town that developed around the Monastery of Rates, established by Henry of Burgundy in 1100 AD on the site of an older temple.
Tribal society	Tribal society refers to societies organized largely on the basis of kinship, especially corporate descent groups. It means a social division within a traditional society consisting of a group of interlinked families or communities sharing a common culture and dialect.
Workforce	The workforce is the labor pool in employment. It is generally used to describe those working for a single company or industry. The term generally excludes the employers or management, and implies those involved in manual labor. It may also mean all those that are available for work.

Addiction	A pattern of behavior characterized by an overwhelming involvement with using a drug and securing its supply is defined as an addiction.
Alcohol abuse	Alcohol abuse, as described in the DSM-IV, is a psychiatric diagnosis describing the use of alcoholic beverages despite negative consequences.
Bureau of Indian Affairs	The Bureau of Indian Affairs is an agency of the federal government of the United States within the Department of the Interior charged with the administration and management of 55.7 million acres of land held in trust by the United States for American Indians, Indian tribes and Alaska Natives. In addition, the Bureau of Indian Affairs provides education services to approximately 48,000 Indians.
Genocide	Genocide is the deliberate and systematic destruction of an ethnic, religious or national group. It is define as "any of the following acts committed with intent to destroy, in whole or in part, a national, ethnical, racial or religious group, as such: killing members of the group; causing serious bodily or mental harm to members of the group; deliberately inflicting on the group conditions of life, calculated to bring about its physical destruction in whole or in part; imposing measures intended to prevent births within the group; forcibly transferring children of the group to another group."
Head Start	Head Start is a program of the United States Department of Health and Human Services that focuses on assisting children from low-income families. Created in 1965, Head Start is the longest-running national school readiness program in the United States. It provides comprehensive education, health, nutrition, and parent involvement services to low-income children and their families.
Indian boarding school	In the late eighteenth century, reformers starting with Washington and Knox, in efforts to "civilize" or otherwise assimilate Native Americans (as opposed to relegating them to reservations), adopted the practice of educating native children in modern American culture. The Civilization Fund Act of 1819 promoted this civilization policy by providing funding to societies (mostly religious) who worked on Native American improvement. An Indian boarding school refers to one of many schools that were established in the United States during the late 19th century to educate Native American youths according to Euro-American standards.
Substance abuse	Substance abuse refers to the overindulgence in and dependence on a psychoactive leading to effects that are detrimental to the individual"s physical health or mental health, or the welfare of others.
Western	The Western is a fiction genre seen in film, television, radio, literature, painting and other visual arts. Westerns are devoted to telling stories set primarily in the later half of the 19th century in what became the Western United States, but also in Western Canada, Mexico, Alaska and even Australia. Some Westerns are set as early as the Battle of the Alamo in 1836 but most are set between the end of the American Civil War and the massacre at Wounded Knee in 1890, though there are several "late Westerns" set as late as the Mexican Revolution in 1913.
Boarding school	A boarding school is a school where some or all pupils not only study, but also live during term time, with their fellow students and possibly teachers.

Casino	A casino is a facility that accommodates certain types of gambling activities. Some are known for hosting live entertainment events, such as concerts and sporting events.
Resource	A resource is any physical or virtual entity of limited availability, or anything used to help one earn a living. In most cases, commercial or even ethic factors require resource allocation through resource management. As resource s are very useful, we attach some information value to them.
Empowerment	Empowerment refers to increasing the spiritual, political, social or economic strength of individuals and communities. Sociological empowerment often addresses members of groups that social discrimination processes have excluded from decision-making processes through - for example - discrimination based on disability, race, ethnicity, religion, or gender.
Future	The future is commonly understood to contain all events that have yet to occur. It is the opposite of the past, and is the time after the present. Organized efforts to predict or forecast the future may have derived from observations by early man of heavenly objects. In physics, which uses a linear conception of time, the future is the portion of the projected time line that is anticipated to occur. In special relativity the future is considered as absolute future or the future light cone. In physics, time is considered to be a fourth dimension
Attachment	In attachment theory psychology, attachment is a product of the activity of a number of behavioral systems that have proximity to a person, e.g. a mother, as a predictable outcome. The concept of there being an "attachment" behavior, stage, and process, to which a growing person remains in proximity to another was developed beginning in 1956 by British developmental psychologist John Bowlby.
Attachment theory	An attachment theory is a coherent group of ideas that attempt to explain attachment, the almost universal human tendency to prefer certain familiar companions over other people, especially in circumstances where the person choosing companions is ill, injured, or distressed in some other way.
Behavior	Behavior refers to the actions or reactions of an object or organism, usually in relation to the environment. Humans evaluate the acceptability of behavior using social norms and regulate behavior by means of social control. In sociology, behavior is considered as having no meaning, being not directed at other people and thus is the most basic human action.
Social learning	The process through which we acquire new information, forms of behavior, or attitudes exclusively or primarily in a social group, is referred to as a social learning.
Social learning theory	A theory emphasizing that boys develop maleness and girls develop femaleness through exposure to scores of influence-including parents, peers, television, and schools-that teach them what it means to be a man or a woman in their culture, is referred to as a social learning theory.

Protective factor	A positive prior factor in an individual"s life that decreases the risk of occurrence of a future delinquent act is called a protective factor.
Importance	Importance is an idea that has existed forever but is being applied very differently in the internet age. It"s a simple cave rules notion relating to ones contribution to a community create some form of their importance in the community. It is the essence of why sites like Wikipedia work.
Coalition	A coalition is an alliance among entities, during which they cooperate in joint action, each in their own self-interest. This alliance may be temporary or a matter of convenience. A coalition thus differs from a more formal covenant.
Child Protective Services	Child Protective Services is the name of a governmental agency in many states in the United States that responds to allegations of child abuse or neglect.
Sexual abuse	Sexual abuse is defined by the forcing of undesired sexual acts by one person to another.
Training	The term training refers to the acquisition of knowledge, skills, and competencies as a result of the teaching of vocational or practical skills and knowledge that relate to specific useful competencies.
Adult	The term adult describes any mature organism, but normally it refers to a human: one that is no longer a child / minor and is now either a man or a woman. It can be defined in terms of biology, law, personal character, or social status. These different aspects are often inconsistent and contradictory.
Relationship	An archaeological Relationship is the position in space and by implication, in time, of an object or context with respect to another. This is determined, not by linear measurement but by determining the sequence of their deposition - which arrived before the other. The key to this is stratigraphy.
Communities	In biological terms, a community is a group of interacting organisms sharing an environment. In human communities, intent, belief, resources, preferences, needs, risks, and a number of other conditions may be present and common, affecting the identity of the participants and their degree of cohesiveness. In sociology, the concept of community has caused infinite debate, and sociologists are yet to reach agreement on a definition of the term.
Group therapy	Group therapy is a form of psychotherapy during which one or several therapists treat a small group of clients together as a group. This may be more cost effective than individual therapy, and possibly even more productive.
Individual	As commonly used, individual refers to a person or to any specific object in a collection. In the 15th century and earlier, and also today within the fields of statistics and metaphysics, individual means "indivisible", typically describing any numerically singular thing, but sometimes meaning "a person.". From the seventeenth century on, individual indicates separateness, as in individualism.

Family therapy	Family therapy is a branch of psychotherapy that works with families and couples in intimate relationships to nurture change and development. It tends to view these in terms of the systems of interaction between family members.
Adolescence	Adolescence (lat adolescere, (to grow) is a transitional stage of physical and mental human development that occurs between childhood and adulthood. This transition involves biological (i.e. pubertal), social, and psychological changes, though the biological or physiological ones are the easiest to measure objectively. Historically, puberty has been heavily associated with teenagers and the onset of adolescent development.[1][2] In recent years, however, the start of puberty has had somewhat of an increase in preAdolescence (particularly females), and Adolescence has had an occasional extension beyond the teenage years (typically males).
Birth control	Birth control is a regimen of one or more actions, devices, or medications followed in order to deliberately prevent or reduce the likelihood of a woman giving birth or becoming pregnant.
Sex	In biology, Sex is a process of combining and mixing genetic traits, often resulting in the specialization of organisms into male and female types (or Sex es.) Sex ual reproduction involves combining specialized cells (gametes) to form offspring that inherit traits from both parents. Gametes can be identical in form and function (known as isogametes), but in many cases an asymmetry has evolved such that two Sex specific types of gametes (heterogametes) exist: male gametes are small, motile, and optimized to transport their genetic information over a distance, while female gametes are large, non-motile and contain the nutrients necessary for the early development of the young organism.
Sex education	Sex education is a broad term used to describe education about human sexual anatomy, sexual reproduction, sexual intercourse, and other aspects of human sexual behavior. Common avenues for sex education are parents or caregivers, school programs, and public health campaigns.
Chinese immigration to the United States	Chinese immigration to the United States mainly consists of three major waves with the first beginning in the early 19th century. For nearly two centuries, the history of Chinese immigration to the United States has witnessed hardship as well as success.
Child maltreatment	Child abuse is the physical or psychological maltreatment of a child by an adult often synonymous with the term child maltreatment or the term child abuse and neglect.
Cooperation	Cooperation is the practice of individuals or larger societal entities working in common with mutually agreed-upon goals and possibly methods, instead of working separately in competition, and in which the success of one is dependent and contingent upon the success of another.
Organization	In sociology organization is understood as planned, coordinated and purposeful action of human beings to construct or compile a common tangible or intangible product or service.
Sex offender	A sex offender is a person who has been criminally charged and convicted of, or has pled guilty to, a sex crime. As a label of identity it is used in criminal psychology.

Sexual orientation	Sexual orientation describes the direction of an individual"s sexuality, often in relation to their own sex or gender. Common terms for describing sexual orientation include bisexual (bi), heterosexual (straight) and homosexual (lesbian/gay).
Advocatus	An Advocatus was generally a medieval term meaning "lawyer". The term was also used in continental Europe as the title of the lay lord charged with the protection and representation in secular matters of an abbey, known more fully as an Advocatus ecclesiae. The office is traceable as early as the beginning of the 5th century in the Roman Empire, the churches being allowed to choose defensores from the body of advocates to represent them in the courts.
Association	Association in archaeology has more than one meaning and is confusing to the layman. Archaeology has been critiqued as a soft science with a somewhat poor standardization of terms. Associated finds or objects refers to a close relationship between two or more objects.
Safety	Safety is the state of being "safe", the condition of being protected against physical, social, spiritual, financial, political, emotional, occupational, psychological, educational or other types or consequences of failure, damage, error, accidents, harm or any other event which could be considered non-desirable.
Corporal punishment	Corporal punishment is the deliberate infliction of pain intended to correct behavior or to punish.
Controversy	A controversy is a matter of opinion over which parties actively disagree, argue, or debate. Controversies can range in size from private disputes between two individuals to large-scale disagreements between societies.
Website	A website (or web site) is a collection of related web pages, images, videos or other digital assets that are addressed with a common domain name or IP address in an Internet Protocol-based network. A web site is hosted on at least one web server, accessible via the Internet or a private local area network. A web page is a document, typically written in plain text interspersed with formatting instructions of Hypertext Markup Language (HTML, XHTML.)

Child	A child is a boy or girl who has not reached puberty, but also refers to offspring of any age.
Welfare	Welfare is financial assistance paid by taxpayers to people who are unable to support themselves. Some welfare is general, while specific and can only be invoked under certain circumstances, such as a scholarship. Individuals may apply for welfare due to disability, lack of education or job training, a low demand for unskilled labor, substance abuse, or an unwillingness to work.
Child Protective Services	Child Protective Services is the name of a governmental agency in many states in the United States that responds to allegations of child abuse or neglect.
Family	A family consists of a domestic group of people, typically affiliated by birth or marriage, or by analogous or comparable relationships — including domestic partnership, cohabitation, adoption, surname and ownership.
Adoption	Adoption is the legal act of permanently placing a child with a parent or parents other than the birth mother or father. An adoption order has the effect of severing the parental responsibilities and rights of the birth parents and transferring those responsibilities and rights onto the adoptive parents.
Assessment	Educational Assessment is the process of documenting, usually in measurable terms, knowledge, skills, attitudes and beliefs. Assessment can focus on the individual learner, the learning community (class, workshop, or other organized group of learners), the institution, or the educational system as a whole. According to the Academic Exchange Quarterly: "Studies of a theoretical or empirical nature (including case studies, portfolio studies, exploratory, or experimental work) addressing the Assessment of learner aptitude and preparation, motivation and learning styles, learning outcomes in achievement and satisfaction in different educational contexts are all welcome, as are studies addressing issues of measurable standards and benchmarks".
Authority	In politics, authority is often used interchangeably with the term "power". However, their meanings differ: while "power" refers to the ability to achieve certain ends, "authority" refers to the legitimacy, justification and right to exercise that power. For example, whilst a mob has the power to punish a criminal, such as through lynching, only the courts have the authority to order capital punishment.
Internet	The Internet is a global system of interconnected computer networks that interchange data by packet switching using the standardized Internet Protocol Suite. It is a "network of networks" that consists of millions of private and public, academic, business, and government networks of local to global scope that are linked by copper wires, fiber-optic cables, wireless connections, and other technologies. The Internet carries various information resources and services, such as electronic mail, online chat, file transfer and file sharing, online gaming, and the inter-linked hypertext documents and other resources of the World Wide Web.
Nature	Nature, in the broadest sense, is equivalent to the natural world, physical universe, material world or material universe. "Nature" refers to the phenomena of the physical world, and also to life in general. Manufactured objects and human interaction generally are not considered part of nature unless qualified in ways such as "human nature" or "the whole of nature".

Software	Computer software, or just software is a general term used to describe a collection of computer programs, procedures and documentation that perform some tasks on a computer system. A screenshot of the OpenOffice.org Writer desktop software The term includes: · Application software such as word processors which perform productive tasks for users, · System software such as operating systems, which interface with hardware to provide the necessary services for application software, and · Middleware which controls and co-ordinates distributed systems. Software includes websites, programs, video games etc. that are coded by programming languages like C, C++, etc. · Firmware which is software programmed resident to electrically programmable memory devices on board mainboards or other types of integrated hardware carriers · Testware which is an umbrella term or container term for all utilities and application software that serve in combination for testing a software package but not necessarily may optionally contribute to operational purposes. As such, testware is not a standing configuration but merely a working environment for application software or subsets thereof. "Software" is sometimes used in a broader context to mean anything which is not hardware but which is used with hardware, such as film, tapes and records. Computer software is often regarded as anything but hardware, meaning that the "hard" are the parts that are tangible while the "soft" part is the intangible objects inside the computer.
Father	The father is defined as the male parent of an offspring. The adjective "paternal" refers to father, parallel to "maternal" for mother. According to the anthropologist Maurice Godelier, the parental role assumed by human males is a critical difference between human society and that of humans" closest biological relatives - chimpanzees and bonobos - who appear to be unaware of their "father" connection.
Mother	A mother is a biological and/or social female parent of an offspring. In the case of a mammal such as a human, the biological mother gestates a fertilized ovum, which is called first an embryo, and then a fetus. This gestation occurs in the mother"s uterus from conception until the fetus is sufficiently developed to be born. The mother then goes into labor and gives birth. Once the child is born, the mother produces milk in a process called lactation to feed the child; often the mother"s breast milk is the child"s sole nourishment for the first year or more of the child"s life.
Single-parent	A Single-parent is a parent who cares for children without the assistance of another person in the home. The legal definition of "single parenthood" may vary according to the local laws of different nations or regions.
Engagement	An engagement is a promise to marry, and also refers to the time between proposal and marriage.

Adoption and Safe Families Act	The Adoption and Safe Families Act was signed into law by President Bill Clinton on November 19, 1997 after having been approved by the United States Congress earlier in the month. It was enacted in an attempt to correct problems that were inherent in the foster care system that deterred the adoption of children with special needs.
Ethics	Ethics, a major branch of philosophy, is the study of values and customs of a person or group. It covers the analysis and employment of concepts such as right and wrong, good and evil, and responsibility. It is divided into three primary areas: meta-ethics, normative ethics, and applied ethics.
Informed consent	Informed consent is a legal condition whereby a person can be said to have given consent based upon an appreciation and understanding of the facts and implications of an action. The individual needs to be in possession of relevant facts and also of his reasoning faculties, such as not being mentally retarded or mentally ill and without an impairment of judgment at the time of consenting.
Quality of life	The quality of life of a population is an important concern in economics and political science. It is measured by many social and economic factors. A large part is standard of living, the amount of money and access to goods and services that a person has; these numbers are fairly easily measured.
Safety	Safety is the state of being "safe", the condition of being protected against physical, social, spiritual, financial, political, emotional, occupational, psychological, educational or other types or consequences of failure, damage, error, accidents, harm or any other event which could be considered non-desirable.
Self-determination	Self-determination is defined as free choice of one"s own acts without external compulsion; and especially as the freedom of the people of a given territory to determine their own political status or independence from their current state. In other words, it is the right of the people of a certain nation to decide how they want to be governed without the influence of any other country. The latter is a complex concept with conflicting definitions and legal criteria for determining which groups may legitimately claim the right to Self-determination..
Client	In ancient Roman society, a Client was a plebeian who was sponsored by a patron benefactor . The patron assisted his Client with his protection and regular gifts; the Client dedicated his vote whenever the patron or his associate was up for election. This right of patronage was established by Romulus, to unite the plebians and the patricians together, in such a manner that one might live without envy, and the other without contempt.
Cross-cultural	Cross-cultural refers to comparative studies based on statistical compilations of cultural data, the term gradually acquired a secondary sense of cultural interactivity. The comparative sense is implied in phrases such as "a cross-cultural perspective," "cross-cultural differences," "a cross-cultural study of..." and so forth, while the interactive signification may be found in works like Attitudes and Adjustment in Cross-Cultural Contact.

Cultural Competence	Cultural competence refers to an ability to interact effectively with people of different cultures.
Culture	Culture generally refers to patterns of human activity and the symbolic structures that give such activity significant importance. Culture has been called "the way of life for an entire society." As such, it includes codes of manners, dress, language, religion, rituals, norms of behavior such as law and morality, and systems of belief.
Social	Social refers to human society or its organization. Although the term is a crucial category in social science and often used in public discourse, its meaning is at times vague, suggesting that it is a fuzzy concept. An added difficulty is that social attributes or relationships may not be directly observable and visible, and must be inferred by abstract thought.
Social Work	Social work is a helping profession focused on social change, problem solving in human relationships and the empowerment and liberation of people to enhance well-being.
Value	Value is a concept that describes the beliefs of an individual or culture. Values are considered subjective and vary across people and cultures. Types of values include ethical/moral values, doctrinal/ideological values, social values, and aesthetic values.
Knowledge	Knowledge is defined variously as expertise, and skills acquired by a person through experience or education; the theoretical or practical understanding of a subject, what is known in a particular field or in total; facts and information or awareness or familiarity gained by experience of a fact or situation. Philosophical debates in general start with Plato"s formulation of knowledge as "justified true belief". There is however no single agreed definition of knowledge presently, nor any prospect of one, and there remain numerous competing theories.
Skill	A skill is the learned capacity to carry out pre-determined results often with the minimum outlay of time, energy, or both. skill s can often be divided into domain-general and domain-specific skill s. For example, in the domain of work, some general skill s would include time management, teamwork and leadership, self motivation and others, whereas domain-specific skill s would be useful only for a certain job.
Child and Family Services	Child and family services are nonprofit organizations designed to better the well being of individuals who come from unfortunate situations, environmental or biological. People who seek or are sought after to participate in these services, usually do not have stable homes and no other resource to turn to. Children might come from abusive or neglectful homes, or live in very poor and dangerous communities.
Temporary Assistance for Needy Families	Temporary Assistance for Needy Families successor to the Aid to Families with Dependent Children program, providing cash assistance to indigent American families with dependent children through the United States Department of Health and Human Services. It is the United States" federal assistance program commonly known as "welfare".

Child advocacy	Child advocacy refers to a range of individuals, professionals and advocacy organizations who promote the optimal development of children. An individual or organization engaging in advocacy typically seeks to protect children"s rights which may be abridged or abused in a number of areas. Rights can be divided into two categories: negative (rights to be free from) and positive (rights to).
Group therapy	Group therapy is a form of psychotherapy during which one or several therapists treat a small group of clients together as a group. This may be more cost effective than individual therapy, and possibly even more productive.
Planning	Planning in organizations and public policy is both the organizational process of creating and maintaining a plan; and the psychological process of thinking about the activities required to create a desired future on some scale.
Guideline	A guideline is any document that aims to streamline particular processes according to a set routine.
Natural	Natural in Archaeology is a term to denote a horizon in the stratigraphic record representing the point from which there is no anthropogenic activity on site and the archaeological record ends. Natural is often the underlying geological makeup of the site and is formed by geological processes. It is the goal of complete excavation to remove the entirety of the archaeological record all the way to "Natural" thus leaving only the Natural deposits of pre human activity on site.
Documentation	Documentation may refer to the process of providing evidence or to the communicable material used to provide such documentation.
Crisis	A crisis may occur on a personal or societal level. It may be a traumatic or stressful change in a person"s life, or an unstable and dangerous social situation, in political, social, economic, military affairs, or a large-scale environmental event, especially one involving an impending abrupt change. More loosely, it is a term meaning "a testing time" or "emergency event".
Welfare reform	Welfare reform is the name for a policy change in countries with a state-administered social welfare system to reduce dependence on welfare, as demanded by political conservatives. A movement to change the federal government"s social welfare policy which shifted responsibility to the states and cut benefits.
Right	In jurisprudence and law, a right is the legal or moral entitlement to do or refrain from doing something or to obtain or refrain from obtaining an action, thing or recognition in civil society. Compare with privilege, or a thing to which one has a just claim. They serve as rules of interaction between people, and, as such, they place constraints and obligations upon the actions of individuals or groups.
Trend	A trend is something that somehow becomes popular within mainstream society over a long period of time. It is the direction of a sequence of events that has some momentum and durability.

Foundation	A Foundation in the United States is a type of charitable organization. However, the Internal Revenue Code distinguishes between private foundations (usually funded by an individual, family, or corporation) and public charities (community foundations and other nonprofit groups that raise money from the general public.) Private foundations have more restrictions and fewer tax benefits than public charities like community foundations.
Website	A website (or web site) is a collection of related web pages, images, videos or other digital assets that are addressed with a common domain name or IP address in an Internet Protocol-based network. A web site is hosted on at least one web server, accessible via the Internet or a private local area network. A web page is a document, typically written in plain text interspersed with formatting instructions of Hypertext Markup Language (HTML, XHTML.)

Legal systems of the world	The three major legal systems of the world today consist of civil law, common law and religious law. However, each country often develops variations on each system or incorporates many other features into the system.
Internet	The Internet is a global system of interconnected computer networks that interchange data by packet switching using the standardized Internet Protocol Suite. It is a "network of networks" that consists of millions of private and public, academic, business, and government networks of local to global scope that are linked by copper wires, fiber-optic cables, wireless connections, and other technologies. The Internet carries various information resources and services, such as electronic mail, online chat, file transfer and file sharing, online gaming, and the inter-linked hypertext documents and other resources of the World Wide Web.
Minor	In law, the term minor is used to refer to a person who is under the age in which one legally assumes adulthood and is legally granted rights afforded to adults in society. Depending on the jurisdiction and application, this age may vary, but is usually marked at either 18 or 21. Specifically, the status of "minor" is defined by the age of majority[
Court	A court is a public forum used by a power base to adjudicate disputes and dispense civil, labor, administrative and criminal justice under its laws. In common law and civil law states, courts are the central means for dispute resolution, and it is generally understood that all persons have an ability to bring their claims before a court. Similarly, those accused of a crime have the right to present their defense before a court.
Philosophy	Philosophy is the discipline concerned with questions of how one should live; what sorts of things exist and what are their essential natures. Though no single definition of philosophy is uncontroversial, and the field has historically expanded and changed depending upon what kinds of questions were interesting or relevant in a given era, it is generally agreed that philosophy is a method, rather than a set of claims, propositions, or theories.
Purpose	Purpose in its most general sense is the anticipated aim which guides action. It is used as the synonym of "goal" and "objective."
Due process	Basic constitutional principle based on the concept of the primacy of the individual and the complementary concept of limitation on governmental power; safeguards the individual from unfair state procedures in judicial or administrative proceedings; due process rights have been extended to juvenile trials.
Court of last resort	In some countries, provinces and states, the court of last resort is the highest court whose rulings cannot be challenged.
Constitutionality	Constitutionality is the condition of acting in accordance with an applicable constitution; the status of a law, a procedure, or an act"s accordance with the laws or guidelines set forth in the applicable constitution. When one of these (laws, procedures, or acts) directly violates the constitution it is unconstitutional. All the rest are considered constitutional until challenged and declared otherwise.

Family	A family consists of a domestic group of people, typically affiliated by birth or marriage, or by analogous or comparable relationships — including domestic partnership, cohabitation, adoption, surname and ownership.
Child	A child is a boy or girl who has not reached puberty, but also refers to offspring of any age.
Role	A role or a social role is a set of connected behaviors, rights and obligations as conceptualized by actors in a social situation. It is an expected behavior in a given individual social status and social position. It is vital to both functionalist and interactionist understandings of society.
Welfare	Welfare is financial assistance paid by taxpayers to people who are unable to support themselves. Some welfare is general, while specific and can only be invoked under certain circumstances, such as a scholarship. Individuals may apply for welfare due to disability, lack of education or job training, a low demand for unskilled labor, substance abuse, or an unwillingness to work.
Adult	The term adult describes any mature organism, but normally it refers to a human: one that is no longer a child / minor and is now either a man or a woman. It can be defined in terms of biology, law, personal character, or social status. These different aspects are often inconsistent and contradictory.
Court of Appeals	Court of Appeals is the title of a court which has the power to consider or hear an appeal. It is also a superior court.
Jurisdiction	In law, jurisdiction is the practical authority granted to a formally constituted legal body or to a political leader to deal with and make pronouncements on legal matters and, by implication, to administer justice within a defined area of responsibility.
Trial court	A trial court is the court in which most civil or criminal cases begin. Not all cases are heard in here; some cases may begin in inferior limited jurisdiction bodies such as the case of the jurisdiction of an administrative body that has been created by statute to make some kind of binding determination under the law and were simplified procedural practices may apply similar to arbitration.
Evidence	Evidence in its broadest sense, refers to anything that is used to determine or demonstrate the truth of an assertion. Philosophically, evidence can include propositions which are presumed to be true used in support of other propositions that are presumed to be falsifiable.
Pregnancy	Pregnancy is the carrying of one or more offspring, known as a fetus or embryo, inside the body of a female mammal such as a human, between conception and birth. In many societies" medical and legal definitions, human pregnancy is somewhat arbitrarily divided into three trimester periods, as a means to simplify reference to the different stages of prenatal development.
Child Protective Services	Child Protective Services is the name of a governmental agency in many states in the United States that responds to allegations of child abuse or neglect.

Welfare reform	Welfare reform is the name for a policy change in countries with a state-administered social welfare system to reduce dependence on welfare, as demanded by political conservatives. A movement to change the federal government"s social welfare policy which shifted responsibility to the states and cut benefits.
Abandonment	Parents that physically leave their children with the intention of completely severing the parent-child relationship are engaging in abandonment. To give up control of a child, legally terminating parental rights; in many states abandonment is considered child abuse.
Abuse	Abuse refers to the use or treatment of something that is seen as harmful. The term can be used for anything ranging from the misuse of a piece of equipment to the severe maltreatment of a person.
Adoption	Adoption is the legal act of permanently placing a child with a parent or parents other than the birth mother or father. An adoption order has the effect of severing the parental responsibilities and rights of the birth parents and transferring those responsibilities and rights onto the adoptive parents.
Delinquent	Delinquent means one who fails to do that which is required by law or by duty when such failure is minor in nature.
Juvenile delinquency	Juvenile delinquency refers to criminal acts performed by juveniles. It may refer to either violent or non-violent crime committed by persons who are under the age of eighteen and are still considered to be a minor. There is much debate about whether or not such a child should be held criminally responsible for his or her own actions.
Status	In sociology or anthropology, social status is the honor or prestige attached to one"s position in society one"s social position. The stratification system, which is the system of distributing rewards to the members of society, determines social status. Social status, the position or rank of a person or group within the stratification system, can be determined two ways. One can earn their social status by their own achievements, which is known as achieved status, or one can be placed in the stratification system by their inherited position, which is called ascribed status.
Status offense	A status offense is an action that is a crime only if the perpetrator is a minor. For instance, consumption of alcohol by a minor may be a status offense in jurisdictions where such consumption is permitted, but only by persons over a specified age.
Sacred Contagion	Sacred Contagion is the belief that spiritual properties within an object, place place usually by direct contact or physical proximity. While the concept of Sacred Contagion has existed in numerous cultures since before recorded history, the term "Sacred Contagion" originated with French sociologist Émile Durkheim, who introduced it in his book The Elementary Forms of Religious Life. An example of Sacred Contagion is chapters 11 through 15 in the Book of Leviticus found in the Bible and Torah.

Software	Computer software, or just software is a general term used to describe a collection of computer programs, procedures and documentation that perform some tasks on a computer system. A screenshot of the OpenOffice.org Writer desktop software The term includes: · Application software such as word processors which perform productive tasks for users, · System software such as operating systems, which interface with hardware to provide the necessary services for application software, and · Middleware which controls and co-ordinates distributed systems. Software includes websites, programs, video games etc. that are coded by programming languages like C, C++, etc. · Firmware which is software programmed resident to electrically programmable memory devices on board mainboards or other types of integrated hardware carriers · Testware which is an umbrella term or container term for all utilities and application software that serve in combination for testing a software package but not necessarily may optionally contribute to operational purposes. As such, testware is not a standing configuration but merely a working environment for application software or subsets thereof. "Software" is sometimes used in a broader context to mean anything which is not hardware but which is used with hardware, such as film, tapes and records. Computer software is often regarded as anything but hardware, meaning that the "hard" are the parts that are tangible while the "soft" part is the intangible objects inside the computer.
African Americans	African Americans are citizens or residents of the United States whose ancestors, usually in predominant part, were indigenous to Sub-Saharan Africa. Most are the descendants of captive Africans who were enslaved within the boundaries of the present United States.
Foster care	Foster care is a system by which a certified, stand-in "parent" cares for minor children or young peoples who have been removed from their birth parents or other custodial adults by state authority. Responsibility for the young person is assumed by the relevant governmental authority and a placement with another family found. There can be voluntary placements by a parent of a child into foster care.
Father	The father is defined as the male parent of an offspring. The adjective "paternal" refers to father, parallel to "maternal" for mother. According to the anthropologist Maurice Godelier, the parental role assumed by human males is a critical difference between human society and that of humans" closest biological relatives - chimpanzees and bonobos - who appear to be unaware of their "father" connection.
Contact	In Family Law, contact is one of the general terms which denotes the level of contact a parent or other significant person in a child"s life can have with that child. Contact forms part of the bundle of rights and privileges which a parent may have in relation to any child of the family.

Child custody	Child custody and guardianship are legal terms which are sometimes used to describe the legal and practical relationship between a parent and his or her child, such as the right of the parent to make decisions for the child, and the parent's duty to care for the child.
Right	In jurisprudence and law, a right is the legal or moral entitlement to do or refrain from doing something or to obtain or refrain from obtaining an action, thing or recognition in civil society. Compare with privilege, or a thing to which one has a just claim. They serve as rules of interaction between people, and, as such, they place constraints and obligations upon the actions of individuals or groups.
Safety	Safety is the state of being "safe", the condition of being protected against physical, social, spiritual, financial, political, emotional, occupational, psychological, educational or other types or consequences of failure, damage, error, accidents, harm or any other event which could be considered non-desirable.
Adolescence	Adolescence (lat adolescere, (to grow) is a transitional stage of physical and mental human development that occurs between childhood and adulthood. This transition involves biological (i.e. pubertal), social, and psychological changes, though the biological or physiological ones are the easiest to measure objectively. Historically, puberty has been heavily associated with teenagers and the onset of adolescent development.[1][2] In recent years, however, the start of puberty has had somewhat of an increase in preAdolescence (particularly females), and Adolescence has had an occasional extension beyond the teenage years (typically males).
Ageing	Ageing is the process of systems" deterioration with time. It is an important part of all human societies reflecting the biological changes that occur, but also reflecting cultural and societal conventions.
Aging out	Aging out is American popular culture vernacular used to describe anytime a youth leaves a formal system of care designed to provide services below a certain age level. There are a variety of applications of the phrase throughout the youth development field. In respect to foster care, Aging out is the process of a youth transitioning from the formal control of the foster care system towards independent living.
Emancipation	Emancipation is a term used to describe various efforts to obtain political rights or equality, often for a specifically disenfranchised group, or more generally in discussion of such matters.
Teenage pregnancy	Teenage pregnancy is defined as an underaged girl becoming pregnant with a baby. While women technically stay in their "teens" until the age of 20, the term is restricted to those under the age threshold of legal adulthood, which is 18 in most of the United States, and 16 in much of the rest of the world.
Procedure	In all lawsuits involving Conflict of Laws, questions of Procedure as opposed to substance are always determined by the lex fori, i.e. the law of the state in which the case is being litigated. This is a part of the process called characterisation. Issues identified as procedural include the following:

· By initiating the action before the forum court, the plaintiff is asking for the grant of the local remedies. This will not be a problem so long as the form of the relief is broadly similar to the relief available under the lex causae, i.e. the law selected under the choice of law rules. But forum courts may refuse a remedy in two situations:

> if the effect of granting the relief sought would offend against the public policy of the forum court;
>
> if the effect of the relief would be so different from that available under the lex causae that it makes the right sought to be enforced a different right. For example, in English law, the court was asked in Phrantzes v Argenti 2 QB 19 to enforce a Greek marriage dowry agreement.

Documentation	Documentation may refer to the process of providing evidence or to the communicable material used to provide such documentation.
Report	In writing, a report is a document characterized by information or other content reflective of inquiry or investigation, which is tailored to the context of a given situation and audience. The purpose of report s is usually to inform. However, report s may include persuasive elements, such as recommendations, suggestions, or other motivating conclusions that indicate possible future actions the report reader might take.
Trend	A trend is something that somehow becomes popular within mainstream society over a long period of time. It is the direction of a sequence of events that has some momentum and durability.
American Bar Association	The American Bar Association is a voluntary bar association of lawyers and law students, which is not specific to any jurisdiction in the United States.
Child Abuse	Child abuse is the physical, sexual, or emotional maltreatment or neglect of children by parents, guardians, or others. Child abuse in its various forms has numerous effects and consequences, both tangible and intangible, upon society, those mistreated, and those entrusted with the responsibility of its detection, prevention and treatment.
Congress	A Congress is a formal meeting of representatives from different countries (or by extension constituent states), or independent organizations (such as different trade unions.) The term Congress was chosen for the United States Congress to emphasize the status of each state represented there as a self-governing unit. Subsequently to the use of Congress by the US legislature, the term has been adopted by many states within unions, and by unitary nation-states in the Americas, to refer to their legislatures.
Federal government	A federal government is the common government of a federation.

The structure of federal government s vary from institution to institution based on a broad definition of a basic federal political system, there are two or more levels of government that exist within an established territory and govern through common institutions with overlapping or shared powers as prescribed by a constitution.

· Government of Australia
· Government of Belgium
· Government of Brazil
· Government of Canada
· Government of Germany
· Government of India
· Government of Malaysia
· Government of Mexico
· Government of Russia
· Government of Switzerland
· Government of the United States

The United States is considered the first modern federation. After declaring independence from Britain, the U.S. adopted its first constitution, the Articles of Confederation in 1781.

Government	A government is a body that has the authority to make and the power to enforce laws within a civil, corporate, religious, academic, or other organization or group.
Judge	A judge is an official who presides over a court. The powers, functions, method of appointment, discipline, and training of a judge vary widely across different jurisdictions.
Evidence-based practice	The term evidence-based practice refers to preferential use of mental and behavioral health interventions for which systematic empirical research has provided evidence of statistically significant effectiveness as treatments for specific problems. It is an approach which tries to specify the way in which professionals or other decision-makers should make decisions by identifying such evidence that there may be for a practice, and rating it according to how scientifically sound it may be. Its goal is to eliminate unsound or excessively risky practices in favour of those that have better outcomes.
Protocol	In international politics, Protocol is the etiquette of diplomacy and affairs of state. A Protocol is a rule which guides how an activity should be performed, especially in the field of diplomacy. In diplomatic services and governmental fields of endeavor protocols are often unwritten guidelines.
Website	A website (or web site) is a collection of related web pages, images, videos or other digital assets that are addressed with a common domain name or IP address in an Internet Protocol-based network. A web site is hosted on at least one web server, accessible via the Internet or a private local area network. A web page is a document, typically written in plain text interspersed with formatting instructions of Hypertext Markup Language (HTML, XHTML.)

Child	A child is a boy or girl who has not reached puberty, but also refers to offspring of any age.
Child Protective Services	Child Protective Services is the name of a governmental agency in many states in the United States that responds to allegations of child abuse or neglect.
Child abuse	Child abuse is the physical, sexual, or emotional maltreatment or neglect of children by parents, guardians, or others. Child abuse in its various forms has numerous effects and consequences, both tangible and intangible, upon society, those mistreated, and those entrusted with the responsibility of its detection, prevention and treatment.
Sexual abuse	Sexual abuse is defined by the forcing of undesired sexual acts by one person to another.
Adoption	Adoption is the legal act of permanently placing a child with a parent or parents other than the birth mother or father. An adoption order has the effect of severing the parental responsibilities and rights of the birth parents and transferring those responsibilities and rights onto the adoptive parents.
Organization	In sociology organization is understood as planned, coordinated and purposeful action of human beings to construct or compile a common tangible or intangible product or service.
Welfare	Welfare is financial assistance paid by taxpayers to people who are unable to support themselves. Some welfare is general, while specific and can only be invoked under certain circumstances, such as a scholarship. Individuals may apply for welfare due to disability, lack of education or job training, a low demand for unskilled labor, substance abuse, or an unwillingness to work.
Abuse	Abuse refers to the use or treatment of something that is seen as harmful. The term can be used for anything ranging from the misuse of a piece of equipment to the severe maltreatment of a person.
African Americans	African Americans are citizens or residents of the United States whose ancestors, usually in predominant part, were indigenous to Sub-Saharan Africa. Most are the descendants of captive Africans who were enslaved within the boundaries of the present United States.
Ethnicity	Ethnicity is a population of human beings whose members identify with each other, either on the basis of a presumed common genealogy or ancestry or recognition by others as a distinct group, or by common cultural, linguistic, religious, or physical traits. The sociologist Max Weber once remarked that "The whole conception of it is so complex and so vague that it might be good to abandon it altogether."
Internet	The Internet is a global system of interconnected computer networks that interchange data by packet switching using the standardized Internet Protocol Suite. It is a "network of networks" that consists of millions of private and public, academic, business, and government networks of local to global scope that are linked by copper wires, fiber-optic cables, wireless connections, and other technologies. The Internet carries various information resources and services, such as electronic mail, online chat, file transfer and file sharing, online gaming, and the inter-linked hypertext documents and other resources of the World Wide Web.

White people	White people is a term which is usually used to refer to human beings characterized, at least in part, by the light pigmentation of their skin. It often refers narrowly to people claiming ancestry exclusively from Europe. A broadly corresponding concept was the Caucasian race.
Race	The term race refers to the concept of dividing people into populations or groups on the basis of various sets of characteristics and beliefs about common ancestry. The most widely used human racial categories are based on visible traits especially skin color, facial features and hair texture, and self-identification.
Statistics	Statistics is a mathematical science pertaining to the collection, analysis, interpretation, and presentation of data. It is applicable to a wide variety of academic disciplines, from the physical and social sciences to the humanities; it is also used and misused for making informed decisions in all areas of business and government.
Software	Computer software, or just software is a general term used to describe a collection of computer programs, procedures and documentation that perform some tasks on a computer system. A screenshot of the OpenOffice.org Writer desktop software The term includes: · Application software such as word processors which perform productive tasks for users, · System software such as operating systems, which interface with hardware to provide the necessary services for application software, and · Middleware which controls and co-ordinates distributed systems. Software includes websites, programs, video games etc. that are coded by programming languages like C, C++, etc. · Firmware which is software programmed resident to electrically programmable memory devices on board mainboards or other types of integrated hardware carriers · Testware which is an umbrella term or container term for all utilities and application software that serve in combination for testing a software package but not necessarily may optionally contribute to operational purposes. As such, testware is not a standing configuration but merely a working environment for application software or subsets thereof. "Software" is sometimes used in a broader context to mean anything which is not hardware but which is used with hardware, such as film, tapes and records. Computer software is often regarded as anything but hardware, meaning that the "hard" are the parts that are tangible while the "soft" part is the intangible objects inside the computer.
Mother	A mother is a biological and/or social female parent of an offspring. In the case of a mammal such as a human, the biological mother gestates a fertilized ovum, which is called first an embryo, and then a fetus. This gestation occurs in the mother"s uterus from conception until the fetus is sufficiently developed to be born. The mother then goes into labor and gives birth. Once the child is born, the mother produces milk in a process called lactation to feed the child; often the mother"s breast milk is the child"s sole nourishment for the first year or more of the child"s life.

Adult	The term adult describes any mature organism, but normally it refers to a human: one that is no longer a child / minor and is now either a man or a woman. It can be defined in terms of biology, law, personal character, or social status. These different aspects are often inconsistent and contradictory.
Experience	Experience as a general concept comprises knowledge of or skill in or observation of some thing or some event gained through involvement in or exposure to that thing or event. The history of the word experience aligns it closely with the concept of experiment.
Authority	In politics, authority is often used interchangeably with the term "power". However, their meanings differ: while "power" refers to the ability to achieve certain ends, "authority" refers to the legitimacy, justification and right to exercise that power. For example, whilst a mob has the power to punish a criminal, such as through lynching, only the courts have the authority to order capital punishment.
Professional	A professional can be either a person in a profession or in sports for payment.
Cruelty	Cruelty can be described as indifference to suffering and even positive pleasure in inflicting it
Historical	((race)) The historical definition of race was an immutable and distinct type or species, sharing distinct racial characteristics such as constitution, temperament, and mental abilities. These races were not conceived as being related with each other, but formed a hierarchy of inherent value called the Great Chain of Being with Europeans usually at the top. As time progressed, Charles Darwin"s theory of evolution was applied to races.
New York	New York is a state in the Mid-Atlantic and Northeastern regions of the United States of America. With 62 counties, it is the country"s third most populous state. It is bordered by Vermont, Massachusetts, Connecticut, New Jersey, and Pennsylvania, and shares a water border with Rhode Island as well as an international border with the Canadian provinces of Quebec and Ontario. Its five largest cities are New York City, Buffalo, Rochester, Yonkers, and Syracuse.
Society	A society is a grouping of individuals, which is characterized by common interest and may have distinctive culture and institutions.
Child Protection	Child protection is used to describe a set of usually government-run services designed to protect children and encourage family stability. These typically include investigation of alleged child abuse, child protective services, foster care, adoption services, and services aimed at supporting at-risk families so they can remain intact. Most children who come to the attention of the child welfare system do so because of any of the following situations, which are often collectively termed child abuse:

· Neglect including the failure to take adequate measures to safeguard a child from harm and/or gross negligence in providing for a child"s basic needs
· Emotional abuse
· Child sexual abuse
· Physical abuse
· Psychological abuse

The United States government"s Administration for Children and Families reported that in 2004 approximately 3.5 million children were involved in investigations of alleged abuse or neglect in the US, while an estimated 872,000 children were determined to have been abused or neglected and an estimated 1,490 children died that year because of abuse or neglect.

The concept of a state sanctioned child welfare system dates back to Plato"s Republic.

Family	A family consists of a domestic group of people, typically affiliated by birth or marriage, or by analogous or comparable relationships — including domestic partnership, cohabitation, adoption, surname and ownership.
Family preservation	Family preservation was the movement to help keep children at home with their families rather than in foster homes or institutions. This movement was a reaction to the earlier policy of family breakup, which pulled children out of unfit homes. Extreme poverty alone was seen as a justified reason to remove children.
Federal government	A federal government is the common government of a federation. The structure of federal government s vary from institution to institution based on a broad definition of a basic federal political system, there are two or more levels of government that exist within an established territory and govern through common institutions with overlapping or shared powers as prescribed by a constitution. · Government of Australia · Government of Belgium · Government of Brazil · Government of Canada · Government of Germany · Government of India · Government of Malaysia · Government of Mexico · Government of Russia · Government of Switzerland · Government of the United States The United States is considered the first modern federation. After declaring independence from Britain, the U.S. adopted its first constitution, the Articles of Confederation in 1781.
Government	A government is a body that has the authority to make and the power to enforce laws within a civil, corporate, religious, academic, or other organization or group.

Violence	*Violence* is the exertion of force with the intent to injure (psychologically or physically) or kill. *Violence* is also used more broadly and metaphorically to describe the destructive action of natural phenomena like storms and earthquakes. Variant uses of the term refer to the destruction of non-living objects
Legislation	Legislation is law which has been promulgated by a legislature or other governing body. The term may refer to a single law, or the collective body of enacted law, while "statute" is also used to refer to a single law. Before an item of legislation becomes law it may be known as a bill, which is typically also known as "legislation" while it remains under active consideration.
State government	A state government is the government of a subnational entity in states with federal forms of government, which shares political power with the federal government or national government. A state government may have some level of political autonomy, or be subject to the direct control of the federal government.
Definition	A definition is a statement of the meaning of a word or phrase. The term to be defined is known as the definiendum. The words which define it are known as the definiens.
Dimension	Dimensions is a French project that makes educational movies about mathematics, focusing on spacial geometry. It uses POV-Ray to render some of the animations, and the films are release under a Creative Commons licence. The fourth chapter, showing the stereographic projection of a polychoron on our three-dimensional space. The film is separated in nine chapters, which follow this plot: · Chapter 1: Dimension two explains Earth"s coordinate system, and introduces the stereographic projection. · Chapter 2: Dimension three discusses how two-dimensional beings would imagine three-dimensional objects. · Chapters 3 and 4: The fourth dimension talk about four-dimensional polytopes, projecting the regular ones stereographically on the three-dimentional space. · Chapters 5 and 6: Complex numbers are about the square root of negative numbers, transformations, and fractals. · Chapters 7 and 8: Fibration show what a fibration is. Complex numbers are used again, and there are circles and tori rotating and being transformed. · Chapter 9: Proof emphasizes the importance of proofs in mathematics, and proves the circle-conservationess of the stereographic projection as an example. .
Corporal punishment	Corporal punishment is the deliberate infliction of pain intended to correct behavior or to punish.
Navajo	Navajo refers or relates to the Navajo people, the second largest Native American tribe in the United States.

Attitude	Attitude is a hypothetical construct that represents an individual"s like or dislike for an item. Attitudes are positive, negative or neutral views of an "attitude object": i.e. a person, behavior or event. People can also be "ambivalent" towards a target, meaning that they simultaneously possess a positive and a negative bias towards the attitude in question.
Culture	Culture generally refers to patterns of human activity and the symbolic structures that give such activity significant importance. Culture has been called "the way of life for an entire society." As such, it includes codes of manners, dress, language, religion, rituals, norms of behavior such as law and morality, and systems of belief.
Discipline	Discipline means to instruct a person or animal to follow a particular code of conduct, or to adhere to a certain "order."
Physical abuse	Physical abuse is abuse involving contact intended to cause pain, injury, or other physical suffering or harm.
Confidentiality	Confidentiality has been defined by the International Organization for Standardization as "ensuring that information is accessible only to those authorized to have access" and is one of the cornerstones of Information security. Confidentiality is one of the design goals for many cryptosystems, made possible in practice by the techniques of modern cryptography.
Child maltreatment	Child abuse is the physical or psychological maltreatment of a child by an adult often synonymous with the term child maltreatment or the term child abuse and neglect.
Report	In writing, a report is a document characterized by information or other content reflective of inquiry or investigation, which is tailored to the context of a given situation and audience. The purpose of report s is usually to inform. However, report s may include persuasive elements, such as recommendations, suggestions, or other motivating conclusions that indicate possible future actions the report reader might take.
Community	A community is a social group of organisms sharing an environment, normally with shared interests. In human communities, intent, belief, resources, preferences, needs, risks and a number of other conditions may be present and common, affecting the identity of the participants and their degree of cohesiveness.
Poverty	Poverty may be seen as the collective condition of poor people, or of poor groups, and in this sense entire nation-states are sometimes regarded as poor. Although the most severe poverty is in the developing world, there is evidence of poverty in every region.

Father	The father is defined as the male parent of an offspring. The adjective "paternal" refers to father, parallel to "maternal" for mother. According to the anthropologist Maurice Godelier, the parental role assumed by human males is a critical difference between human society and that of humans" closest biological relatives - chimpanzees and bonobos - who appear to be unaware of their "father" connection.
Single-parent	A Single-parent is a parent who cares for children without the assistance of another person in the home. The legal definition of "single parenthood" may vary according to the local laws of different nations or regions.
Addiction	A pattern of behavior characterized by an overwhelming involvement with using a drug and securing its supply is defined as an addiction.
Alcohol abuse	Alcohol abuse, as described in the DSM-IV, is a psychiatric diagnosis describing the use of alcoholic beverages despite negative consequences.
Cycle of violence	The term cycle of violence refers to repeated acts of violence between groups as a cyclical pattern, associated with high emotions and doctrines retribution, revenge, such as "an eye for an eye."
Substance abuse	Substance abuse refers to the overindulgence in and dependence on a psychoactive leading to effects that are detrimental to the individual"s physical health or mental health, or the welfare of others.
Court	A court is a public forum used by a power base to adjudicate disputes and dispense civil, labor, administrative and criminal justice under its laws. In common law and civil law states, courts are the central means for dispute resolution, and it is generally understood that all persons have an ability to bring their claims before a court. Similarly, those accused of a crime have the right to present their defense before a court.
Employment	Employment is a contract between two parties, one being the employer and the other being the employee. An employee may be defined as: "A person in the service of another under any contract of hire, express or implied, oral or written, where the employer has the power or right to control and direct the employee in the material details of how the work is to be performed."
Adoption and Safe Families Act	The Adoption and Safe Families Act was signed into law by President Bill Clinton on November 19, 1997 after having been approved by the United States Congress earlier in the month. It was enacted in an attempt to correct problems that were inherent in the foster care system that deterred the adoption of children with special needs.
Animal abuse	Animal abuse is defined as any act that contributes to the physical, psychological, or emotional pain, suffering, or death of an animal, or that otherwise threatens its welfare. The act may involve active maltreatment or passive neglect or omission and may be direct or indirect.

Human	A Human is a member of a species of bipedal primates in the family Hominidae . DNA and fossil evidence indicates that modern Human s originated in east Africa about 200,000 years ago. When compared to other animals and primates, Human s have a highly developed brain, capable of abstract reasoning, language, introspection and problem solving.
Post traumatic stress disorder	Post traumatic stress disorder is an anxiety disorder that can develop after exposure to one or more terrifying events in which grave physical harm occurred or was threatened.
Violence Against Women Act	The Violence Against Women Act of 1994 is a United States federal law. It was passed as Title IV, sec. 40001-40703 of the Violent Crime Control and Law Enforcement Act of 1994 HR 3355 and signed as Public Law 103-322 by President Bill Clinton on September 13, 1994. It provided $1.6 billion to enhance investigation and prosecution of the violent crime perpetrated against women, increased pre-trial detention of the accused, imposed automatic and mandatory restitution on those convicted, and allowed civil redress in cases prosecutors chose to leave unprosecuted.
Women	A woman is a female human. The term woman irregular plural: women usually is used for an adult, with the term girl being the usual term for a female child or adolescent. However, the term woman is also sometimes used to identify a female human, regardless of age, as in phrases such as "Women"s rights".
Domestic violence	Domestic violence occurs when a family member, partner or ex-partner attempts to physically or psychologically dominate another. Domestic violence often refers to violence between spouses, or spousal abuse but can also include cohabitants and non-married intimate partners. Domestic violence occurs in all cultures; people of all races, ethnicities, religions, sexes and classes can be perpetrators of domestic violence. Domestic violence is perpetrated by both men and women.
Stress	Stress is the consequence of the failure to adapt to change. Less simply: it is the condition that results when person-environment transactions lead the individual to perceive a discrepancy, whether real or not, between the demands of a situation and the resources of the person"s biological, psychological or social systems.
Expulsion	Expulsion at a school or university is defined as removing a student from the institution for violating rules or honor codes. If a child has been expelled from two schools then a state school is legally permitted to refuse to admit a pupil ; in the case of a school which is on special measures then a child who has been expelled from one school may be treated in this way. Because of these rules if a child is expelled from a school then it can result in them being removed totally from the state education system.
Munchausen syndrome by proxy	Munchausen Syndrome by Proxy refers to insidious disorders in which injury is deliberately and gradually inflicted upon a person usually for gaining attention or some other benefit.

Sexual orientation	Sexual orientation describes the direction of an individual"s sexuality, often in relation to their own sex or gender. Common terms for describing sexual orientation include bisexual (bi), heterosexual (straight) and homosexual (lesbian/gay).
Shaken baby syndrome	Shaken baby syndrome is a form of child abuse affecting between 1,200 and 1,600 children every year in the USA. It encompasses a variety of outcomes that are attributed to shaking an infant or small child.
Need	A Need is something that is necessary for humans to live a healthy life. Need s are distinguished from wants because a deficiency would cause a clear negative outcome, such as dysfunction or death. Need s can be objective and physical, such as food and water, or they can be subjective and psychological, such as the Need for self-esteem.
From each according to his ability, to each according to his need	From each according to his ability, to each according to his need is a slogan popularized by Karl Marx in his 1875 Critique of the Gotha Program. The phrase summarizes the principles that, under a communist system, every person should contribute to society to the best of his ability and consume from society in proportion to his needs, regardless of how much he has contributed. In the Marxist view, such an arrangement will be made possible by the abundance of goods and services that a developed communist society will produce; the idea is that there will be enough to satisfy everyone"s needs.
Ageing	Ageing is the process of systems" deterioration with time. It is an important part of all human societies reflecting the biological changes that occur, but also reflecting cultural and societal conventions.
Exploitation	In political economy, economics, and sociology, exploitation involves a persistent social relationship in which certain persons are being mistreated or unfairly used for the benefit of others. This corresponds to one ethical conception of exploitation, that is, the treatment of human beings as mere means to an end — or as mere "objects".
Gender	Gender refers to the differences between men and women. Gender identity is an individual"s self-conception as being male or female, as distinguished from actual biological sex. In general, gender often refers to purely social rather than biological differences.
Incest	Incest is defined as sexual intercourse or any form of sexual activity between closely related persons, especially within the nuclear family
Legal systems of the world	The three major legal systems of the world today consist of civil law, common law and religious law. However, each country often develops variations on each system or incorporates many other features into the system.
Abandonment	Parents that physically leave their children with the intention of completely severing the parent-child relationship are engaging in abandonment.To give up control of a child, legally terminating parental rights; in many states abandonment is considered child abuse.

Social	Social refers to human society or its organization. Although the term is a crucial category in social science and often used in public discourse, its meaning is at times vague, suggesting that it is a fuzzy concept. An added difficulty is that social attributes or relationships may not be directly observable and visible, and must be inferred by abstract thought.
Social work	Social work is a helping profession focused on social change, problem solving in human relationships and the empowerment and liberation of people to enhance well-being.
Ritualism	Outward conformity to norms without a commitment to values they support is ritualism.
Survivor	Survivor is a popular reality television game show format produced in many countries throughout the world. In the show, contestants are isolated in the wilderness and compete for cash and other prizes. The show uses a progressive elimination, allowing the contestants to vote off a tribe member, until only one final contestant remains and wins the title of "Sole Survivor". The format for Survivor was created in 1992 by Charlie Parsons, and the first production of it was the Swedish show Expedition: Robinson in 1997.
Congress of Racial Equality	The Congress of Racial Equality is a U.S. civil rights organization that played a pivotal role in the Civil Rights Movement from its foundation to the mid-1960s. The group"s inspiration was Krishnalal Shridharani"s book War Without Violence, which outlined Gandhi"s step-by-step procedures for organizing people and mounting a nonviolent campaign.
Association	Association in archaeology has more than one meaning and is confusing to the layman. Archaeology has been critiqued as a soft science with a somewhat poor standardization of terms. Associated finds or objects refers to a close relationship between two or more objects.
Crisis	A crisis may occur on a personal or societal level. It may be a traumatic or stressful change in a person"s life, or an unstable and dangerous social situation, in political, social, economic, military affairs, or a large-scale environmental event, especially one involving an impending abrupt change. More loosely, it is a term meaning "a testing time" or "emergency event".
Disposition	A Disposition is a habit, a preparation, a state of readiness, or a tendency to act in a specified way. The terms Disposition al belief and occurrent belief refer, in the former case, to a belief that is held in the mind but not currently being considered, and in the latter case, to a belief that is currently being considered by the mind. In Bourdieu"s theory of fields Disposition s are the natural tendencies of each individual to take on a certain position in any field.
Intake	Intake refers to process during which a juvenile referral is received and a decision is made to file a petition in juvenile court to release the juvenile, to place the juvenile under supervision, or to refer the juvenile elsewhere.

Public	Public is about the what of belonging to the people; relating to, or affecting, a nation, state, or community; opposed to private; as, the public treasury, a road or lake. Public is also defined as the people of a nation not affiliated with the government of that nation.
Right	In jurisprudence and law, a right is the legal or moral entitlement to do or refrain from doing something or to obtain or refrain from obtaining an action, thing or recognition in civil society. Compare with privilege, or a thing to which one has a just claim. They serve as rules of interaction between people, and, as such, they place constraints and obligations upon the actions of individuals or groups.
Decision making	Decision making can be regarded as an outcome of mental processes leading to the selection of a course of action among several alternatives.
Evidence	Evidence in its broadest sense, refers to anything that is used to determine or demonstrate the truth of an assertion. Philosophically, evidence can include propositions which are presumed to be true used in support of other propositions that are presumed to be falsifiable.
Risk	Risk is a concept that denotes the precise probability of specific eventualities. Technically, the notion of Risk is independent from the notion of value and, as such, eventualities may have both beneficial and adverse consequences. However, in general usage the convention is to focus only on potential negative impact to some characteristic of value that may arise from a future event.
Risk factor	A risk factor is a variable associated with an increased risk of disease or infection. risk factor s are correlational and not necessarily causal, because correlation does not imply causation. For example, being young cannot be said to cause measles, but young people are more at risk as they are less likely to have developed immunity during a previous epidemic.
Safety	Safety is the state of being "safe", the condition of being protected against physical, social, spiritual, financial, political, emotional, occupational, psychological, educational or other types or consequences of failure, damage, error, accidents, harm or any other event which could be considered non-desirable.
Native Americans	Native Americans in the United States are the indigenous peoples from the regions of North America now encompassed by the continental United States, including parts of Alaska. They comprise a large number of distinct tribes, states, and ethnic groups, many of which are still enduring as political communities.
Foster care	Foster care is a system by which a certified, stand-in "parent" cares for minor children or young peoples who have been removed from their birth parents or other custodial adults by state authority. Responsibility for the young person is assumed by the relevant governmental authority and a placement with another family found. There can be voluntary placements by a parent of a child into foster care.

Victimology	Victimology is the study of why certain people are victims of crime and how lifestyles affect the chances that a certain person will fall victim to a crime. The field can cover a wide number of disciplines, including sociology, psychology, criminal justice, law and advocacy.
American Humane Association	The American Humane Association is an organization founded in 1877 dedicated to the welfare of animals and children.
Committee	A committee is a type of small deliberative assembly that is usually subordinate to another, larger deliberative assembly.
Trend	A trend is something that somehow becomes popular within mainstream society over a long period of time. It is the direction of a sequence of events that has some momentum and durability.
American Bar Association	The American Bar Association is a voluntary bar association of lawyers and law students, which is not specific to any jurisdiction in the United States.
Website	A website (or web site) is a collection of related web pages, images, videos or other digital assets that are addressed with a common domain name or IP address in an Internet Protocol-based network. A web site is hosted on at least one web server, accessible via the Internet or a private local area network. A web page is a document, typically written in plain text interspersed with formatting instructions of Hypertext Markup Language (HTML, XHTML.)

Addiction	A pattern of behavior characterized by an overwhelming involvement with using a drug and securing its supply is defined as an addiction.
Alcohol abuse	Alcohol abuse, as described in the DSM-IV, is a psychiatric diagnosis describing the use of alcoholic beverages despite negative consequences.
Family	A family consists of a domestic group of people, typically affiliated by birth or marriage, or by analogous or comparable relationships — including domestic partnership, cohabitation, adoption, surname and ownership.
Family preservation	Family preservation was the movement to help keep children at home with their families rather than in foster homes or institutions. This movement was a reaction to the earlier policy of family breakup, which pulled children out of unfit homes. Extreme poverty alone was seen as a justified reason to remove children.
Father	The father is defined as the male parent of an offspring. The adjective "paternal" refers to father, parallel to "maternal" for mother. According to the anthropologist Maurice Godelier, the parental role assumed by human males is a critical difference between human society and that of humans" closest biological relatives - chimpanzees and bonobos - who appear to be unaware of their "father" connection.
Mother	A mother is a biological and/or social female parent of an offspring. In the case of a mammal such as a human, the biological mother gestates a fertilized ovum, which is called first an embryo, and then a fetus. This gestation occurs in the mother"s uterus from conception until the fetus is sufficiently developed to be born. The mother then goes into labor and gives birth. Once the child is born, the mother produces milk in a process called lactation to feed the child; often the mother"s breast milk is the child"s sole nourishment for the first year or more of the child"s life.
Substance abuse	Substance abuse refers to the overindulgence in and dependence on a psychoactive leading to effects that are detrimental to the individual"s physical health or mental health, or the welfare of others.
Adoption	Adoption is the legal act of permanently placing a child with a parent or parents other than the birth mother or father. An adoption order has the effect of severing the parental responsibilities and rights of the birth parents and transferring those responsibilities and rights onto the adoptive parents.
Employment	Employment is a contract between two parties, one being the employer and the other being the employee. An employee may be defined as: "A person in the service of another under any contract of hire, express or implied, oral or written, where the employer has the power or right to control and direct the employee in the material details of how the work is to be performed."
Experience	Experience as a general concept comprises knowledge of or skill in or observation of some thing or some event gained through involvement in or exposure to that thing or event. The history of the word experience aligns it closely with the concept of experiment.

Child	A child is a boy or girl who has not reached puberty, but also refers to offspring of any age.
Federal government	A federal government is the common government of a federation. The structure of federal government s vary from institution to institution based on a broad definition of a basic federal political system, there are two or more levels of government that exist within an established territory and govern through common institutions with overlapping or shared powers as prescribed by a constitution. · Government of Australia · Government of Belgium · Government of Brazil · Government of Canada · Government of Germany · Government of India · Government of Malaysia · Government of Mexico · Government of Russia · Government of Switzerland · Government of the United States The United States is considered the first modern federation. After declaring independence from Britain, the U.S. adopted its first constitution, the Articles of Confederation in 1781.
Government	A government is a body that has the authority to make and the power to enforce laws within a civil, corporate, religious, academic, or other organization or group.
Internet	The Internet is a global system of interconnected computer networks that interchange data by packet switching using the standardized Internet Protocol Suite. It is a "network of networks" that consists of millions of private and public, academic, business, and government networks of local to global scope that are linked by copper wires, fiber-optic cables, wireless connections, and other technologies. The Internet carries various information resources and services, such as electronic mail, online chat, file transfer and file sharing, online gaming, and the inter-linked hypertext documents and other resources of the World Wide Web.
State government	A state government is the government of a subnational entity in states with federal forms of government, which shares political power with the federal government or national government. A state government may have some level of political autonomy, or be subject to the direct control of the federal government.
Welfare	Welfare is financial assistance paid by taxpayers to people who are unable to support themselves. Some welfare is general, while specific and can only be invoked under certain circumstances, such as a scholarship. Individuals may apply for welfare due to disability, lack of education or job training, a low demand for unskilled labor, substance abuse, or an unwillingness to work.

Controversies	Controversy is a state of prolonged public dispute or debate, usually concerning a matter of opinion, but , as in the controversy between evolutionary biology and Creationism or Intelligent Design. Sam Cooper coined the word circa 1384 from Latin controversia, as a composite of controversus - "turned in an opposite direction," from contra - "against" - and vertere - to turn, or versus , hence, "to turn against." Benford"s law of controversy, as expressed by science-fiction author Gregory Benford in 1980, states: "Passion is inversely proportional to the amount of real (true) information available." In other words, the fewer facts are known to and agreed on by the participants, the more controversy there is, and the more is known the less controversy there is. Thus, for example, controversies in physics are limited to areas where experiments cannot be carried out yet, while all of economics is in continuous controversy, because, in stark contrast, none of its mathematical models accurately and predictably represents reality.
Evidence-based practice	The term evidence-based practice refers to preferential use of mental and behavioral health interventions for which systematic empirical research has provided evidence of statistically significant effectiveness as treatments for specific problems. It is an approach which tries to specify the way in which professionals or other decision-makers should make decisions by identifying such evidence that there may be for a practice, and rating it according to how scientifically sound it may be. Its goal is to eliminate unsound or excessively risky practices in favour of those that have better outcomes.
Adoption and Safe Families Act	The Adoption and Safe Families Act was signed into law by President Bill Clinton on November 19, 1997 after having been approved by the United States Congress earlier in the month. It was enacted in an attempt to correct problems that were inherent in the foster care system that deterred the adoption of children with special needs.
Resource	A resource is any physical or virtual entity of limited availability, or anything used to help one earn a living. In most cases, commercial or even ethic factors require resource allocation through resource management. As resource s are very useful, we attach some information value to them.
Personal and cultural value	A personal and cultural value is a relative ethic value, an assumption upon which implementation can be extrapolated. A value system is a set of consistent values and measures. A principle value is a foundation upon which other values and measures of integrity are based.
Crisis	A crisis may occur on a personal or societal level. It may be a traumatic or stressful change in a person"s life, or an unstable and dangerous social situation, in political, social, economic, military affairs, or a large-scale environmental event, especially one involving an impending abrupt change. More loosely, it is a term meaning "a testing time" or "emergency event".
Social	Social refers to human society or its organization. Although the term is a crucial category in social science and often used in public discourse, its meaning is at times vague, suggesting that it is a fuzzy concept. An added difficulty is that social attributes or relationships may not be directly observable and visible, and must be inferred by abstract thought.

Social learning	The process through which we acquire new information, forms of behavior, or attitudes exclusively or primarily in a social group, is referred to as a social learning.
Social learning theory	A theory emphasizing that boys develop maleness and girls develop femaleness through exposure to scores of influence-including parents, peers, television, and schools-that teach them what it means to be a man or a woman in their culture, is referred to as a social learning theory.
Base	Base and Superstructure constitute the dialectical synthetic pair that is explicitly and implicitly common to every form of socialism. As used by Karl Marx, the pair function as a gestalt for the figure of a given stage of a human culture and the ground of its mode of production and distinguishes the basis of social orders from other, formative and persisting, social conditions. In Marxist theory, human society consists of two economic parts: the Base and the Superstructure; the Base comprehends the relations of production -- employer-employee work conditions, the technical division of labour, and property relations -- into which people enter to produce the necessities and amenities of life.
Perspective	Perspective in theory of cognition is the choice of a context or a reference or the result of this choice from which to sense, categorize, measure or codify experience, cohesively forming a coherent belief, typically for comparing with another. One may further recognize a number of subtly distinctive meanings, close to those of paradigm, point of view, reality tunnel, umwelt, or weltanschauung.
Teamwork	Teamwork is the concept of people working together cooperatively, as in a sports team
Domestic violence	Domestic violence occurs when a family member, partner or ex-partner attempts to physically or psychologically dominate another. Domestic violence often refers to violence between spouses, or spousal abuse but can also include cohabitants and non-married intimate partners. Domestic violence occurs in all cultures; people of all races, ethnicities, religions, sexes and classes can be perpetrators of domestic violence. Domestic violence is perpetrated by both men and women.
Mental health	Mental health is a term used to describe either a level of cognitive or emotional wellbeing or an absence of a mental disorder.
Violence	*Violence* is the exertion of force with the intent to injure (psychologically or physically) or kill. *Violence* is also used more broadly and metaphorically to describe the destructive action of natural phenomena like storms and earthquakes. Variant uses of the term refer to the destruction of non-living objects
Need	A Need is something that is necessary for humans to live a healthy life. Need s are distinguished from wants because a deficiency would cause a clear negative outcome, such as dysfunction or death. Need s can be objective and physical, such as food and water, or they can be subjective and psychological, such as the Need for self-esteem.

From each according to his ability, to each according to his need	From each according to his ability, to each according to his need is a slogan popularized by Karl Marx in his 1875 Critique of the Gotha Program. The phrase summarizes the principles that, under a communist system, every person should contribute to society to the best of his ability and consume from society in proportion to his needs, regardless of how much he has contributed. In the Marxist view, such an arrangement will be made possible by the abundance of goods and services that a developed communist society will produce; the idea is that there will be enough to satisfy everyone"s needs.
Right	In jurisprudence and law, a right is the legal or moral entitlement to do or refrain from doing something or to obtain or refrain from obtaining an action, thing or recognition in civil society. Compare with privilege, or a thing to which one has a just claim. They serve as rules of interaction between people, and, as such, they place constraints and obligations upon the actions of individuals or groups.
Court	A court is a public forum used by a power base to adjudicate disputes and dispense civil, labor, administrative and criminal justice under its laws. In common law and civil law states, courts are the central means for dispute resolution, and it is generally understood that all persons have an ability to bring their claims before a court. Similarly, those accused of a crime have the right to present their defense before a court.
Judge	A judge is an official who presides over a court. The powers, functions, method of appointment, discipline, and training of a judge vary widely across different jurisdictions.
Minor	In law, the term minor is used to refer to a person who is under the age in which one legally assumes adulthood and is legally granted rights afforded to adults in society. Depending on the jurisdiction and application, this age may vary, but is usually marked at either 18 or 21. Specifically, the status of "minor" is defined by the age of majority[
Protocol	In international politics, Protocol is the etiquette of diplomacy and affairs of state. A Protocol is a rule which guides how an activity should be performed, especially in the field of diplomacy. In diplomatic services and governmental fields of endeavor protocols are often unwritten guidelines.
Child Protective Services	Child Protective Services is the name of a governmental agency in many states in the United States that responds to allegations of child abuse or neglect.
Child abuse	Child abuse is the physical, sexual, or emotional maltreatment or neglect of children by parents, guardians, or others. Child abuse in its various forms has numerous effects and consequences, both tangible and intangible, upon society, those mistreated, and those entrusted with the responsibility of its detection, prevention and treatment.

Adult	The term adult describes any mature organism, but normally it refers to a human: one that is no longer a child / minor and is now either a man or a woman. It can be defined in terms of biology, law, personal character, or social status. These different aspects are often inconsistent and contradictory.
Sexual abuse	Sexual abuse is defined by the forcing of undesired sexual acts by one person to another.
Temporary Assistance for Needy Families	Temporary Assistance for Needy Families successor to the Aid to Families with Dependent Children program, providing cash assistance to indigent American families with dependent children through the United States Department of Health and Human Services. It is the United States" federal assistance program commonly known as "welfare".
African Americans	African Americans are citizens or residents of the United States whose ancestors, usually in predominant part, were indigenous to Sub-Saharan Africa. Most are the descendants of captive Africans who were enslaved within the boundaries of the present United States.
Cultural competence	Cultural competence refers to an ability to interact effectively with people of different cultures.
Gay	Gay usually describes a person"s sexual orientation, being the standard term for homosexual. Gay sometimes also refers to commonalities shared by homosexual people, as in "gay history", the ideological concept of a hypothetical gay culture, as in "gay music." The word gay is sometimes used to refer to same-sex relationships.
Native Americans	Native Americans in the United States are the indigenous peoples from the regions of North America now encompassed by the continental United States, including parts of Alaska. They comprise a large number of distinct tribes, states, and ethnic groups, many of which are still enduring as political communities.
Lesbian	A lesbian is a woman who is romantically and sexually attracted only to other women. Some women in same-sex relationships do not identify as lesbian, but as bisexual, queer, or another label. As with any interpersonal activity, sexual expression depends on the context of the relationship.
Group therapy	Group therapy is a form of psychotherapy during which one or several therapists treat a small group of clients together as a group. This may be more cost effective than individual therapy, and possibly even more productive.
Loneliness	Loneliness is an emotional state in which a person or animal experiences a powerful feeling of emptiness and isolation.
Aid	Aid is the help, mostly economic, which may be provided to communities or countries in the event of a humanitarian crisis or to achieve a socioeconomic objective. Humanitarian aid is therefore primarily used for emergency relief, while development aid aims to create long-term sustainable economic growth. Wealthier countries typically provide aid to economically developing countries.

Head Start	Head Start is a program of the United States Department of Health and Human Services that focuses on assisting children from low-income families. Created in 1965, Head Start is the longest-running national school readiness program in the United States. It provides comprehensive education, health, nutrition, and parent involvement services to low-income children and their families.
Client	In ancient Roman society, a Client was a plebeian who was sponsored by a patron benefactor . The patron assisted his Client with his protection and regular gifts; the Client dedicated his vote whenever the patron or his associate was up for election. This right of patronage was established by Romulus, to unite the plebians and the patricians together, in such a manner that one might live without envy, and the other without contempt.
Empowerment	Empowerment refers to increasing the spiritual, political, social or economic strength of individuals and communities. Sociological empowerment often addresses members of groups that social discrimination processes have excluded from decision-making processes through - for example - discrimination based on disability, race, ethnicity, religion, or gender.
Kinship	Kinship is a relationship between any entities that share a genealogical origin, through either biological, cultural, or historical descent. In anthropology the kinship system includes people related both by descent and marriage, while usage in biology includes descent and mating. Human kinship relations through marriage are commonly called "affinity" in contrast to "descent" also called "consanguinity", although the two may overlap in marriages among those of common descent. Family relations as sociocultural genealogy lead back to gods
Hurricane	A hurricane is one of many meteorological terms for a storm system characterized by a low pressure center and thunderstorms that produces strong wind and flooding rain. It feeds on the heat released when moist air rises and the water vapor it contains condenses.
Hurricane Katrina	Hurricane Katrina was the costliest and one of the five deadliest hurricanes in the history of the United States. It was the sixth-strongest Atlantic hurricane ever recorded and the third-strongest hurricane on record that made landfall in the United States. Katrina formed on August 23 during the 2005 Atlantic hurricane season and caused devastation along much of the north-central Gulf Coast. The most severe loss of life and property damage occurred in New Orleans, Louisiana, which flooded as the levee system catastrophically failed, in many cases hours after the storm had moved inland.
New Zealand	New Zealand has a modern, prosperous, developed economy with an estimated GDP of $106 billion. The country has a high standard of living with GDP per capita estimated at $26,000. The tertiary sector is the largest sector in the economy 67.6% of GDP, followed by the secondary sector 27.8% of GDP and the primary sector 4.7% of GDP. It is heavily dependent on trade, particularly in agricultural products, and exports account for almost 28% of its output.
Sacred Contagion	Sacred Contagion is the belief that spiritual properties within an object, place place usually by direct contact or physical proximity. While the concept of Sacred Contagion has existed in numerous cultures since before recorded history, the term "Sacred Contagion" originated with French sociologist Émile Durkheim, who introduced it in his book The Elementary Forms of Religious Life.

An example of Sacred Contagion is chapters 11 through 15 in the Book of Leviticus found in the Bible and Torah.

Decision making	Decision making can be regarded as an outcome of mental processes leading to the selection of a course of action among several alternatives.

Phase	A phase is one part or portion in recurring or serial activities or occurrences logically connected within a greater process, often resulting in an output or a change. Phase or phases may also refer to:

· Phase problem, the loss of information from a physical measurement
· Phase, a physically distinctive form of a substance, such as the solid, liquid, and gaseous states of ordinary matter
· Phase transition is the transformation of a thermodynamic system from one phase to another
· The initial condition of a cyclic phenomenon

· Phase, initial angle of a sinusoid function at its origin
· Continuous Fourier transform, angle of a complex coefficient representing the phase of one sinusoidal component
· The current state of a cyclic phenomenon

· Lunar phase, the appearance of the Moon as viewed from the Earth
· Planetary phase, the appearance of the illuminated section of a planet
· Instantaneous phase, generalization for both cyclic and non-cyclic phenomena
· Phase factor, a complex scalar in the context of quantum mechanics
· Polyphase system, a means of distributing alternating current electric power in multiple conducting wires with definite phase offsets

· Single-phase electric power
· Three-phase electric power Basics of three-phase electric power
· Three-phase Mathematics of three-phase electric power
· In biology, a part of the cell cycle in which cells divide and reproduce
· Phaser, an audio effect.
· Archaeological phase, a discrete period of occupation at an archaeological site.

· "Phases", an episode of the TV series Buffy the Vampire Slayer
· Phases, fictional boss monsters from the .hack franchise
· Phase, an incarnation of the DC Comics character usually known as Phantom Girl
· Phase IV, a 1974 science fiction movie directed by Saul Bass

· A phase is a musical composition using Steve Reich"s phasing technique.
· Phase, a syntactic domain hypothesized by Noam Chomsky
· Phase 10, a card game created by Fundex Games
· Phase, a music game for the iPod developed by Harmonix Music Systems
· Phase usually a period of combat within a larger military operation .

American Association of Retired Persons	American Association of Retired Persons, is a United States-based non-government organization. According to its mission statement, it is "a nonprofit, nonpartisan membership organization for people age 50 and over ... dedicated to enhancing quality of life for all as we age," which "provides a wide range of unique benefits, special products, and services for our members."
Association	Association in archaeology has more than one meaning and is confusing to the layman. Archaeology has been critiqued as a soft science with a somewhat poor standardization of terms. Associated finds or objects refers to a close relationship between two or more objects.
Extended family	Extended family refers to a family group consisting of more than two generations of the same kinship line living either within the same household or, more usually in the west, very close to one another.
Legal systems of the world	The three major legal systems of the world today consist of civil law, common law and religious law. However, each country often develops variations on each system or incorporates many other features into the system.
Abandonment	Parents that physically leave their children with the intention of completely severing the parent-child relationship are engaging in abandonment. To give up control of a child, legally terminating parental rights; in many states abandonment is considered child abuse.
Foster care	Foster care is a system by which a certified, stand-in "parent" cares for minor children or young peoples who have been removed from their birth parents or other custodial adults by state authority. Responsibility for the young person is assumed by the relevant governmental authority and a placement with another family found. There can be voluntary placements by a parent of a child into foster care.
Subsidy	In economics, a subsidy is a type of financial government assistance, such as a grant, tax break, or trade barrier, in order to encourage the production or purchase of a good. The term subsidy may also refer to assistance granted by others, such as individuals or non-government institutions.
Assessment	Educational Assessment is the process of documenting, usually in measurable terms, knowledge, skills, attitudes and beliefs. Assessment can focus on the individual learner, the learning community (class, workshop, or other organized group of learners), the institution, or the educational system as a whole. According to the Academic Exchange Quarterly: "Studies of a theoretical or empirical nature (including case studies, portfolio studies, exploratory, or experimental work) addressing the Assessment of learner aptitude and preparation, motivation and learning styles, learning outcomes in achievement and satisfaction in different educational contexts are all welcome, as are studies addressing issues of measurable standards and benchmarks".

California	The State of California is the most populated state of the United States of America. Located on the Pacific coast of North America, it is bordered by Oregon, Nevada and Arizona in the United States, and Baja California in Mexico. The state"s four largest cities are Los Angeles, San Diego, San Jose and San Francisco. California is known for its diverse climate and ethnically diverse population. The state has 58 counties.
Trend	A trend is something that somehow becomes popular within mainstream society over a long period of time. It is the direction of a sequence of events that has some momentum and durability.
American Humane Association	The American Humane Association is an organization founded in 1877 dedicated to the welfare of animals and children.
Human	A Human is a member of a species of bipedal primates in the family Hominidae . DNA and fossil evidence indicates that modern Human s originated in east Africa about 200,000 years ago. When compared to other animals and primates, Human s have a highly developed brain, capable of abstract reasoning, language, introspection and problem solving.
Website	A website (or web site) is a collection of related web pages, images, videos or other digital assets that are addressed with a common domain name or IP address in an Internet Protocol-based network. A web site is hosted on at least one web server, accessible via the Internet or a private local area network. A web page is a document, typically written in plain text interspersed with formatting instructions of Hypertext Markup Language (HTML, XHTML.)

Foster care	Foster care is a system by which a certified, stand-in "parent" cares for minor children or young peoples who have been removed from their birth parents or other custodial adults by state authority. Responsibility for the young person is assumed by the relevant governmental authority and a placement with another family found. There can be voluntary placements by a parent of a child into foster care.
Addiction	A pattern of behavior characterized by an overwhelming involvement with using a drug and securing its supply is defined as an addiction.
African Americans	African Americans are citizens or residents of the United States whose ancestors, usually in predominant part, were indigenous to Sub-Saharan Africa. Most are the descendants of captive Africans who were enslaved within the boundaries of the present United States.
Alcohol abuse	Alcohol abuse, as described in the DSM-IV, is a psychiatric diagnosis describing the use of alcoholic beverages despite negative consequences.
Employment	Employment is a contract between two parties, one being the employer and the other being the employee. An employee may be defined as: "A person in the service of another under any contract of hire, express or implied, oral or written, where the employer has the power or right to control and direct the employee in the material details of how the work is to be performed."
Family	A family consists of a domestic group of people, typically affiliated by birth or marriage, or by analogous or comparable relationships — including domestic partnership, cohabitation, adoption, surname and ownership.
Adoption	Adoption is the legal act of permanently placing a child with a parent or parents other than the birth mother or father. An adoption order has the effect of severing the parental responsibilities and rights of the birth parents and transferring those responsibilities and rights onto the adoptive parents.
Analysis	Analysis is the process of breaking a complex topic or substance into smaller parts to gain a better understanding of it. The technique has been applied in the study of mathematics and logic since before Aristotle, though analysis as a formal concept is a relatively recent development. As a formal concept, the method has variously been ascribed by Ibn al-Haytham, Descartes, Galileo, and Isaac Newton, as a practical method of physical discovery.
Cooperative	A cooperative is an autonomous association of persons united voluntarily to meet their common economic, social, and cultural needs and aspirations through a jointly-owned and democratically-controlled enterprise.

Faith-based initiatives	Faith-based initiatives is a department under the Office of the President of the United States that was established by President George W. Bush through executive order on January 29, 2001, and which represents one of the key domestic policies of Bush"s campaign promise of "compassionate conservatism." The initiative seeks to strengthen faith-based and community organizations and expand their capacity to provide federally-funded social services, with the idea being that these groups are well-situated to meet the needs of local individuals. As Texas governor Bush had used the "Charitable Choice" provisions of the 1996 welfare reform which allowed "faith-based" entities to compete for government contracts to deliver social services to support faith-based groups in Texas.
Native Americans	Native Americans in the United States are the indigenous peoples from the regions of North America now encompassed by the continental United States, including parts of Alaska. They comprise a large number of distinct tribes, states, and ethnic groups, many of which are still enduring as political communities.
Public	Public is about the what of belonging to the people; relating to, or affecting, a nation, state, or community; opposed to private; as, the public treasury, a road or lake. Public is also defined as the people of a nation not affiliated with the government of that nation.
Welfare	Welfare is financial assistance paid by taxpayers to people who are unable to support themselves. Some welfare is general, while specific and can only be invoked under certain circumstances, such as a scholarship. Individuals may apply for welfare due to disability, lack of education or job training, a low demand for unskilled labor, substance abuse, or an unwillingness to work.
White people	White people is a term which is usually used to refer to human beings characterized, at least in part, by the light pigmentation of their skin. It often refers narrowly to people claiming ancestry exclusively from Europe. A broadly corresponding concept was the Caucasian race.
Ageing	Ageing is the process of systems" deterioration with time. It is an important part of all human societies reflecting the biological changes that occur, but also reflecting cultural and societal conventions.
Child	A child is a boy or girl who has not reached puberty, but also refers to offspring of any age.
Gender	Gender refers to the differences between men and women. Gender identity is an individual"s self-conception as being male or female, as distinguished from actual biological sex. In general, gender often refers to purely social rather than biological differences.
Race	The term race refers to the concept of dividing people into populations or groups on the basis of various sets of characteristics and beliefs about common ancestry. The most widely used human racial categories are based on visible traits especially skin color, facial features and hair texture, and self-identification.

Statistics	Statistics is a mathematical science pertaining to the collection, analysis, interpretation, and presentation of data. It is applicable to a wide variety of academic disciplines, from the physical and social sciences to the humanities; it is also used and misused for making informed decisions in all areas of business and government.
Historical	((race)) The historical definition of race was an immutable and distinct type or species, sharing distinct racial characteristics such as constitution, temperament, and mental abilities. These races were not conceived as being related with each other, but formed a hierarchy of inherent value called the Great Chain of Being with Europeans usually at the top. As time progressed, Charles Darwin"s theory of evolution was applied to races.
Almshouses	Almshouses are charitable housing provided to enable people typically elderly people who can no longer work to earn enough to pay rent to live in a particular community. They are often targeted at the poor of a locality, at those from certain forms of previous employment, or their widows, and are generally maintained by a charity or the trustees of a bequest.
Orphan train	Orphan train refers to a practice of the Children"s Aid Society in which urban youths were sent west on trains for adoption with local farm couples.
Orphanage	An orphanage is an institution dedicated to caring for orphans and abused, abandoned, and neglected children. Largely seen as an inferior alternative to family-based childcare such as some forms of foster care, adoption, community-based care and other family-based child-care, they may be privately or publicly funded, and many are run by religious organizations.
Welfare reform	Welfare reform is the name for a policy change in countries with a state-administered social welfare system to reduce dependence on welfare, as demanded by political conservatives. A movement to change the federal government"s social welfare policy which shifted responsibility to the states and cut benefits.
Reformism	Socialist Reformism is the belief that gradual democratic changes in a society can ultimately change a society"s fundamental economic relations and political structures. This belief grew out of opposition to revolutionary socialism, which contends that revolutions are necessary to fundamentally change a society.
Planning	Planning in organizations and public policy is both the organizational process of creating and maintaining a plan; and the psychological process of thinking about the activities required to create a desired future on some scale.
Adoption and Safe Families Act	The Adoption and Safe Families Act was signed into law by President Bill Clinton on November 19, 1997 after having been approved by the United States Congress earlier in the month. It was enacted in an attempt to correct problems that were inherent in the foster care system that deterred the adoption of children with special needs.

Family preservation	Family preservation was the movement to help keep children at home with their families rather than in foster homes or institutions. This movement was a reaction to the earlier policy of family breakup, which pulled children out of unfit homes. Extreme poverty alone was seen as a justified reason to remove children.
Kinship	Kinship is a relationship between any entities that share a genealogical origin, through either biological, cultural, or historical descent. In anthropology the kinship system includes people related both by descent and marriage, while usage in biology includes descent and mating. Human kinship relations through marriage are commonly called "affinity" in contrast to "descent" also called "consanguinity", although the two may overlap in marriages among those of common descent. Family relations as sociocultural genealogy lead back to gods
Personal Responsibility and Work Opportunity Reconciliation Act	The Personal Responsibility and Work Opportunity Reconciliation Act of 1996 is a United States federal law considered to be a fundamental shift in both the method and goal of federal cash assistance to the poor.
Quality of life	The quality of life of a population is an important concern in economics and political science. It is measured by many social and economic factors. A large part is standard of living, the amount of money and access to goods and services that a person has; these numbers are fairly easily measured.
Child and Family Services	Child and family services are nonprofit organizations designed to better the well being of individuals who come from unfortunate situations, environmental or biological. People who seek or are sought after to participate in these services, usually do not have stable homes and no other resource to turn to. Children might come from abusive or neglectful homes, or live in very poor and dangerous communities.
Security	Security is the condition of being protected against danger or loss.
Social	Social refers to human society or its organization. Although the term is a crucial category in social science and often used in public discourse, its meaning is at times vague, suggesting that it is a fuzzy concept. An added difficulty is that social attributes or relationships may not be directly observable and visible, and must be inferred by abstract thought.
Social Security	Social security primarily refers to social welfare service concerned with social protection, or protection against socially recognized conditions, including poverty, old age, disability, unemployment and others.
Aid	Aid is the help, mostly economic, which may be provided to communities or countries in the event of a humanitarian crisis or to achieve a socioeconomic objective. Humanitarian aid is therefore primarily used for emergency relief, while development aid aims to create long-term sustainable economic growth. Wealthier countries typically provide aid to economically developing countries.

Aid for Dependent Children	Aid for Dependent Children was a federal assistance program, which was administered by the United States Department of Health and Human Services. Criticisms of it included there were relatively lax time limitations for participation in the program; that the program encouraged child birth to trigger or prolong benefits, and the suggestion that this had a dysgenic effect on the US population; and there were few incentives to join or rejoin the workforce, as entry level jobs could not provide the standard of living provided by it.
Dependent	The dependent variables are those that are observed to change in response to the independent variables.
Federal government	A federal government is the common government of a federation. The structure of federal government s vary from institution to institution based on a broad definition of a basic federal political system, there are two or more levels of government that exist within an established territory and govern through common institutions with overlapping or shared powers as prescribed by a constitution. · Government of Australia · Government of Belgium · Government of Brazil · Government of Canada · Government of Germany · Government of India · Government of Malaysia · Government of Mexico · Government of Russia · Government of Switzerland · Government of the United States The United States is considered the first modern federation. After declaring independence from Britain, the U.S. adopted its first constitution, the Articles of Confederation in 1781.
Government	A government is a body that has the authority to make and the power to enforce laws within a civil, corporate, religious, academic, or other organization or group.
Evidence-based practice	The term evidence-based practice refers to preferential use of mental and behavioral health interventions for which systematic empirical research has provided evidence of statistically significant effectiveness as treatments for specific problems. It is an approach which tries to specify the way in which professionals or other decision-makers should make decisions by identifying such evidence that there may be for a practice, and rating it according to how scientifically sound it may be. Its goal is to eliminate unsound or excessively risky practices in favour of those that have better outcomes.
Role	A role or a social role is a set of connected behaviors, rights and obligations as conceptualized by actors in a social situation. It is an expected behavior in a given individual social status and social position. It is vital to both functionalist and interactionist understandings of society.

Independence	Independence is the self-government of a nation, country, or state by its residents and population, or some portion thereof, generally exercising sovereignty.
Child advocacy	Child advocacy refers to a range of individuals, professionals and advocacy organizations who promote the optimal development of children. An individual or organization engaging in advocacy typically seeks to protect children"s rights which may be abridged or abused in a number of areas. Rights can be divided into two categories: negative (rights to be free from) and positive (rights to).
State government	A state government is the government of a subnational entity in states with federal forms of government, which shares political power with the federal government or national government. A state government may have some level of political autonomy, or be subject to the direct control of the federal government.
Youth	Youth is defined by as, "The time of life when one is young; especially: a: the period between childhood and maturity b: the early period of existence, growth, or development."
Internet	The Internet is a global system of interconnected computer networks that interchange data by packet switching using the standardized Internet Protocol Suite. It is a "network of networks" that consists of millions of private and public, academic, business, and government networks of local to global scope that are linked by copper wires, fiber-optic cables, wireless connections, and other technologies. The Internet carries various information resources and services, such as electronic mail, online chat, file transfer and file sharing, online gaming, and the inter-linked hypertext documents and other resources of the World Wide Web.
Trust	Trust is a relationship of reliance. A trusted party is presumed to seek to fulfill policies, ethical codes, law and their previous promises.
Legal systems of the world	The three major legal systems of the world today consist of civil law, common law and religious law. However, each country often develops variations on each system or incorporates many other features into the system.
Temporary Assistance for Needy Families	Temporary Assistance for Needy Families successor to the Aid to Families with Dependent Children program, providing cash assistance to indigent American families with dependent children through the United States Department of Health and Human Services. It is the United States" federal assistance program commonly known as "welfare".
Abandonment	Parents that physically leave their children with the intention of completely severing the parent-child relationship are engaging in abandonment.To give up control of a child, legally terminating parental rights; in many states abandonment is considered child abuse.

Assessment	Educational Assessment is the process of documenting, usually in measurable terms, knowledge, skills, attitudes and beliefs. Assessment can focus on the individual learner, the learning community (class, workshop, or other organized group of learners), the institution, or the educational system as a whole. According to the Academic Exchange Quarterly: "Studies of a theoretical or empirical nature (including case studies, portfolio studies, exploratory, or experimental work) addressing the Assessment of learner aptitude and preparation, motivation and learning styles, learning outcomes in achievement and satisfaction in different educational contexts are all welcome, as are studies addressing issues of measurable standards and benchmarks".
Software	Computer software, or just software is a general term used to describe a collection of computer programs, procedures and documentation that perform some tasks on a computer system. A screenshot of the OpenOffice.org Writer desktop software
	The term includes:
	· Application software such as word processors which perform productive tasks for users, · System software such as operating systems, which interface with hardware to provide the necessary services for application software, and · Middleware which controls and co-ordinates distributed systems. Software includes websites, programs, video games etc. that are coded by programming languages like C, C++, etc.
	· Firmware which is software programmed resident to electrically programmable memory devices on board mainboards or other types of integrated hardware carriers · Testware which is an umbrella term or container term for all utilities and application software that serve in combination for testing a software package but not necessarily may optionally contribute to operational purposes. As such, testware is not a standing configuration but merely a working environment for application software or subsets thereof. "Software" is sometimes used in a broader context to mean anything which is not hardware but which is used with hardware, such as film, tapes and records. Computer software is often regarded as anything but hardware, meaning that the "hard" are the parts that are tangible while the "soft" part is the intangible objects inside the computer.
Agency	Agency is an area of commercial law dealing with a contractual or quasi-contractual tripartite, or non-contractual set of relationships when an Agent is authorized to act on behalf of another to create a legal relationship with a Third Party. Succinctly, it may be referred to as the relationship between a principal and an agent whereby the principal, expressly or impliedly, authorizes the agent to work under his control and on his behalf. The agent is, thus, required to negotiate on behalf of the principal or bring him and third parties into contractual relationship.
Behavior	Behavior refers to the actions or reactions of an object or organism, usually in relation to the environment. Humans evaluate the acceptability of behavior using social norms and regulate behavior by means of social control. In sociology, behavior is considered as having no meaning, being not directed at other people and thus is the most basic human action.

Behavior modification	Behavior modification is the use of empirically demonstrated behavior change techniques to improve behavior, such as altering an individual"s behaviors and reactions to stimuli through positive and negative reinforcement of adaptive behavior and/or the reduction of maladaptive behavior through positive and negative punishment.
Group home	A Group home is a structure designed or converted to serve as a non-secure home for persons who share a common characteristic. In the United States, the term most often refers to homes designed for those in need of social assistance, and who are usually deemed incapable of living alone or without proper supervision.
Association	Association in archaeology has more than one meaning and is confusing to the layman. Archaeology has been critiqued as a soft science with a somewhat poor standardization of terms. Associated finds or objects refers to a close relationship between two or more objects.
Ethics	Ethics, a major branch of philosophy, is the study of values and customs of a person or group. It covers the analysis and employment of concepts such as right and wrong, good and evil, and responsibility. It is divided into three primary areas: meta-ethics, normative ethics, and applied ethics.
Education	Education encompasses teaching and learning specific skills, and also something less tangible but more profound: the imparting of knowledge, positive judgement and well-developed wisdom. Education has as one of its fundamental aspects the imparting of culture from generation to generation.
Professional	A professional can be either a person in a profession or in sports for payment.
Training	The term training refers to the acquisition of knowledge, skills, and competencies as a result of the teaching of vocational or practical skills and knowledge that relate to specific useful competencies.
Lanham Act	The Lanham Act is a piece of legislation that contains the federal statutes of trademark law in the United States.
Father	The father is defined as the male parent of an offspring. The adjective "paternal" refers to father, parallel to "maternal" for mother. According to the anthropologist Maurice Godelier, the parental role assumed by human males is a critical difference between human society and that of humans" closest biological relatives - chimpanzees and bonobos - who appear to be unaware of their "father" connection.
Mother	A mother is a biological and/or social female parent of an offspring. In the case of a mammal such as a human, the biological mother gestates a fertilized ovum, which is called first an embryo, and then a fetus. This gestation occurs in the mother"s uterus from conception until the fetus is sufficiently developed to be born. The mother then goes into labor and gives birth. Once the child is born, the mother produces milk in a process called lactation to feed the child; often the mother"s breast milk is the child"s sole nourishment for the first year or more of the child"s life.

Single-parent	A Single-parent is a parent who cares for children without the assistance of another person in the home. The legal definition of "single parenthood" may vary according to the local laws of different nations or regions.
Authority	In politics, authority is often used interchangeably with the term "power". However, their meanings differ: while "power" refers to the ability to achieve certain ends, "authority" refers to the legitimacy, justification and right to exercise that power. For example, whilst a mob has the power to punish a criminal, such as through lynching, only the courts have the authority to order capital punishment.
Conflict	Conflict is actual or perceived opposition of needs, values and interests. A Conflict can be internal (within oneself) or external (between two or more individuals.) Conflict as a concept can help explain many aspects of social life such as social disagreement, Conflict s of interests, and fights between individuals, groups, or organizations.
Teamwork	Teamwork is the concept of people working together cooperatively, as in a sports team
Resource	A resource is any physical or virtual entity of limited availability, or anything used to help one earn a living. In most cases, commercial or even ethic factors require resource allocation through resource management. As resource s are very useful, we attach some information value to them.
Caregiver	Caregiver are normally used to refer to unpaid relatives or friends who support people with disabilities. The words may be prefixed with "Family" "Spousal" or "Child" to distinguish between different care situations. Terms such as "Voluntary caregiver" and "Informal carer" are also used occasionally, but these terms have been criticized by carers as misnomers because they are perceived as belittling the huge impact that caring may have on an individual"s life, the lack of realistic alternatives, and the degree of perceived duty of care felt by many relatives.
Media	In communication, media are the storage and transmission tools used to store and deliver information or data. It is often referred to as synonymous with mass media or news media, but may refer to a single medium used to communicate any data for any purpose.
Managed Care	The term "managed care" is used to describe a variety of techniques intended to reduce the cost of providing health benefits and improve the quality of care "managed care techniques", organizations that use those techniques or provide them as services to other organizations "managed care organizations", or systems of financing and delivering health care to enrollees organized around managed care techniques and concepts "managed care delivery systems". According to the National Library of Medicine,
Privatization	Privatization is the transfer of ownership from the public sector to the private sector. A transfer in the opposite direction could be referred to the nationalization or municipalization of some property or responsibility.

Trend	A trend is something that somehow becomes popular within mainstream society over a long period of time. It is the direction of a sequence of events that has some momentum and durability.
Minority	A minority is a sociological group that does not constitute a politically dominant plurality of the total population of a given society. A sociological minority is not necessarily a numerical minority it may include any group that is disadvantaged with respect to a dominant group in terms of social status, education, employment, wealth and political power.
Sacred Contagion	Sacred Contagion is the belief that spiritual properties within an object, place place usually by direct contact or physical proximity. While the concept of Sacred Contagion has existed in numerous cultures since before recorded history, the term "Sacred Contagion" originated with French sociologist Émile Durkheim, who introduced it in his book The Elementary Forms of Religious Life. An example of Sacred Contagion is chapters 11 through 15 in the Book of Leviticus found in the Bible and Torah.
Class action	In law, the class action is a procedural device used in litigation to determine the rights of and remedies, if any, for large numbers of people whose cases involve common questions of law and/or fact.
Right	In jurisprudence and law, a right is the legal or moral entitlement to do or refrain from doing something or to obtain or refrain from obtaining an action, thing or recognition in civil society. Compare with privilege, or a thing to which one has a just claim. They serve as rules of interaction between people, and, as such, they place constraints and obligations upon the actions of individuals or groups.
Litigation	Litigation is an 18th and 19th century form of dispute resolution based upon the medieval Anglo-Saxon practice of jousting. In the 20th century in America, alternative dispute resolution methods began to take precedence, including arbitration and mediation.
Title IV	Title IV of the Higher Education Act of 1965 (the Act, the HSA) covers the administration of the United States federal student financial aid programs. American colleges and universities are generally classified with regard to their inclusion under Title IV, such as under the U.S. Department of Education statistics .
Data Analysis	Qualitative data analysis QDA or qualitative research is the analysis of non-numerical data, for example words, photographs, observations, etc..
Organization	In sociology organization is understood as planned, coordinated and purposeful action of human beings to construct or compile a common tangible or intangible product or service.
Website	A website (or web site) is a collection of related web pages, images, videos or other digital assets that are addressed with a common domain name or IP address in an Internet Protocol-based network. A web site is hosted on at least one web server, accessible via the Internet or a private local area network.

A web page is a document, typically written in plain text interspersed with formatting instructions of Hypertext Markup Language (HTML, XHTML.)

African Americans	African Americans are citizens or residents of the United States whose ancestors, usually in predominant part, were indigenous to Sub-Saharan Africa. Most are the descendants of captive Africans who were enslaved within the boundaries of the present United States.
Child	A child is a boy or girl who has not reached puberty, but also refers to offspring of any age.
Child advocacy	Child advocacy refers to a range of individuals, professionals and advocacy organizations who promote the optimal development of children. An individual or organization engaging in advocacy typically seeks to protect children"s rights which may be abridged or abused in a number of areas. Rights can be divided into two categories: negative (rights to be free from) and positive (rights to).
Foster care	Foster care is a system by which a certified, stand-in "parent" cares for minor children or young peoples who have been removed from their birth parents or other custodial adults by state authority. Responsibility for the young person is assumed by the relevant governmental authority and a placement with another family found. There can be voluntary placements by a parent of a child into foster care.
Reform	A reform movement is a kind of social movement that aims to make gradual change, or change in certain aspects of society rather than rapid or fundamental changes.
Reformism	Socialist Reformism is the belief that gradual democratic changes in a society can ultimately change a society"s fundamental economic relations and political structures. This belief grew out of opposition to revolutionary socialism, which contends that revolutions are necessary to fundamentally change a society.
Role	A role or a social role is a set of connected behaviors, rights and obligations as conceptualized by actors in a social situation. It is an expected behavior in a given individual social status and social position. It is vital to both functionalist and interactionist understandings of society.
Welfare	Welfare is financial assistance paid by taxpayers to people who are unable to support themselves. Some welfare is general, while specific and can only be invoked under certain circumstances, such as a scholarship. Individuals may apply for welfare due to disability, lack of education or job training, a low demand for unskilled labor, substance abuse, or an unwillingness to work.
Welfare reform	Welfare reform is the name for a policy change in countries with a state-administered social welfare system to reduce dependence on welfare, as demanded by political conservatives. A movement to change the federal government"s social welfare policy which shifted responsibility to the states and cut benefits.
Adoption	Adoption is the legal act of permanently placing a child with a parent or parents other than the birth mother or father. An adoption order has the effect of severing the parental responsibilities and rights of the birth parents and transferring those responsibilities and rights onto the adoptive parents.

Adoption and Safe Families Act	The Adoption and Safe Families Act was signed into law by President Bill Clinton on November 19, 1997 after having been approved by the United States Congress earlier in the month. It was enacted in an attempt to correct problems that were inherent in the foster care system that deterred the adoption of children with special needs.
Family	A family consists of a domestic group of people, typically affiliated by birth or marriage, or by analogous or comparable relationships — including domestic partnership, cohabitation, adoption, surname and ownership.
Ageing	Ageing is the process of systems" deterioration with time. It is an important part of all human societies reflecting the biological changes that occur, but also reflecting cultural and societal conventions.
Aging out	Aging out is American popular culture vernacular used to describe anytime a youth leaves a formal system of care designed to provide services below a certain age level. There are a variety of applications of the phrase throughout the youth development field. In respect to foster care, Aging out is the process of a youth transitioning from the formal control of the foster care system towards independent living.
Decision making	Decision making can be regarded as an outcome of mental processes leading to the selection of a course of action among several alternatives.
Right	In jurisprudence and law, a right is the legal or moral entitlement to do or refrain from doing something or to obtain or refrain from obtaining an action, thing or recognition in civil society. Compare with privilege, or a thing to which one has a just claim. They serve as rules of interaction between people, and, as such, they place constraints and obligations upon the actions of individuals or groups.
Federal government	A federal government is the common government of a federation. The structure of federal government s vary from institution to institution based on a broad definition of a basic federal political system, there are two or more levels of government that exist within an established territory and govern through common institutions with overlapping or shared powers as prescribed by a constitution. · Government of Australia · Government of Belgium · Government of Brazil · Government of Canada · Government of Germany · Government of India · Government of Malaysia · Government of Mexico · Government of Russia · Government of Switzerland · Government of the United States

	The United States is considered the first modern federation. After declaring independence from Britain, the U.S. adopted its first constitution, the Articles of Confederation in 1781.
Government	A government is a body that has the authority to make and the power to enforce laws within a civil, corporate, religious, academic, or other organization or group.
Evidence-based practice	The term evidence-based practice refers to preferential use of mental and behavioral health interventions for which systematic empirical research has provided evidence of statistically significant effectiveness as treatments for specific problems. It is an approach which tries to specify the way in which professionals or other decision-makers should make decisions by identifying such evidence that there may be for a practice, and rating it according to how scientifically sound it may be. Its goal is to eliminate unsound or excessively risky practices in favour of those that have better outcomes.
Child Protective Services	Child Protective Services is the name of a governmental agency in many states in the United States that responds to allegations of child abuse or neglect.
Cultural competence	Cultural competence refers to an ability to interact effectively with people of different cultures.
Internet	The Internet is a global system of interconnected computer networks that interchange data by packet switching using the standardized Internet Protocol Suite. It is a "network of networks" that consists of millions of private and public, academic, business, and government networks of local to global scope that are linked by copper wires, fiber-optic cables, wireless connections, and other technologies. The Internet carries various information resources and services, such as electronic mail, online chat, file transfer and file sharing, online gaming, and the inter-linked hypertext documents and other resources of the World Wide Web.
Planning	Planning in organizations and public policy is both the organizational process of creating and maintaining a plan; and the psychological process of thinking about the activities required to create a desired future on some scale.
Assessment	Educational Assessment is the process of documenting, usually in measurable terms, knowledge, skills, attitudes and beliefs. Assessment can focus on the individual learner, the learning community (class, workshop, or other organized group of learners), the institution, or the educational system as a whole. According to the Academic Exchange Quarterly: "Studies of a theoretical or empirical nature (including case studies, portfolio studies, exploratory, or experimental work) addressing the Assessment of learner aptitude and preparation, motivation and learning styles, learning outcomes in achievement and satisfaction in different educational contexts are all welcome, as are studies addressing issues of measurable standards and benchmarks".
Contact	In Family Law, contact is one of the general terms which denotes the level of contact a parent or other significant person in a child"s life can have with that child. Contact forms part of the bundle of rights and privileges which a parent may have in relation to any child of the family.

Father	The father is defined as the male parent of an offspring. The adjective "paternal" refers to father, parallel to "maternal" for mother. According to the anthropologist Maurice Godelier, the parental role assumed by human males is a critical difference between human society and that of humans" closest biological relatives - chimpanzees and bonobos - who appear to be unaware of their "father" connection.
Legal systems of the world	The three major legal systems of the world today consist of civil law, common law and religious law. However, each country often develops variations on each system or incorporates many other features into the system.
Mother	A mother is a biological and/or social female parent of an offspring. In the case of a mammal such as a human, the biological mother gestates a fertilized ovum, which is called first an embryo, and then a fetus. This gestation occurs in the mother"s uterus from conception until the fetus is sufficiently developed to be born. The mother then goes into labor and gives birth. Once the child is born, the mother produces milk in a process called lactation to feed the child; often the mother"s breast milk is the child"s sole nourishment for the first year or more of the child"s life.
Single-parent	A Single-parent is a parent who cares for children without the assistance of another person in the home. The legal definition of "single parenthood" may vary according to the local laws of different nations or regions.
Abandonment	Parents that physically leave their children with the intention of completely severing the parent-child relationship are engaging in abandonment.To give up control of a child, legally terminating parental rights; in many states abandonment is considered child abuse.
Abuse	Abuse refers to the use or treatment of something that is seen as harmful. The term can be used for anything ranging from the misuse of a piece of equipment to the severe maltreatment of a person.
Authority	In politics, authority is often used interchangeably with the term "power". However, their meanings differ: while "power" refers to the ability to achieve certain ends, "authority" refers to the legitimacy, justification and right to exercise that power. For example, whilst a mob has the power to punish a criminal, such as through lynching, only the courts have the authority to order capital punishment.
Collaboration	Collaboration is a structured, recursive process where two or more people work together toward a common goal—typically an intellectual endeavor that is creative in nature—by sharing knowledge, learning and building consensus.
Kinship	Kinship is a relationship between any entities that share a genealogical origin, through either biological, cultural, or historical descent. In anthropology the kinship system includes people related both by descent and marriage, while usage in biology includes descent and mating. Human kinship relations through marriage are commonly called "affinity" in contrast to "descent" also called "consanguinity", although the two may overlap in marriages among those of common descent. Family relations as sociocultural genealogy lead back to gods

Overview	An overview in policy debate is part of a speech which is flagged as not responding to the line-by-line arguments on the flow. An overview may be "global" if presented at the beginning of a speech or "local" if presented at the beginning of a position.
Structured interview	A structured interview is a quantitative research method commonly employed in survey research. The aim of this approach is to ensure that each interviewee is presented with exactly the same questions in the same order. This ensures that answers can be reliably aggregated and that comparisons can be made with confidence between sample subgroups or between different survey periods.
Child and Family Services	Child and family services are nonprofit organizations designed to better the well being of individuals who come from unfortunate situations, environmental or biological. People who seek or are sought after to participate in these services, usually do not have stable homes and no other resource to turn to. Children might come from abusive or neglectful homes, or live in very poor and dangerous communities.
Agency	Agency is an area of commercial law dealing with a contractual or quasi-contractual tripartite, or non-contractual set of relationships when an Agent is authorized to act on behalf of another to create a legal relationship with a Third Party. Succinctly, it may be referred to as the relationship between a principal and an agent whereby the principal, expressly or impliedly, authorizes the agent to work under his control and on his behalf. The agent is, thus, required to negotiate on behalf of the principal or bring him and third parties into contractual relationship.
Natural	Natural in Archaeology is a term to denote a horizon in the stratigraphic record representing the point from which there is no anthropogenic activity on site and the archaeological record ends. Natural is often the underlying geological makeup of the site and is formed by geological processes. It is the goal of complete excavation to remove the entirety of the archaeological record all the way to "Natural" thus leaving only the Natural deposits of pre human activity on site.
Teamwork	Teamwork is the concept of people working together cooperatively, as in a sports team
Individual	As commonly used, individual refers to a person or to any specific object in a collection. In the 15th century and earlier, and also today within the fields of statistics and metaphysics, individual means "indivisible", typically describing any numerically singular thing, but sometimes meaning "a person.". From the seventeenth century on, individual indicates separateness, as in individualism.
Information sharing	The term "Information sharing" gained popularity as a result of the 9/11 Commission Hearings and its report of the United States government"s lack of response to information known about the planned terrorist attack on the New York City World Trade Center prior to the event. The resulting commission testimony led to the enactment of several executive orders by President Bush that mandated agencies implement policies to "share information" across organizational boundaries. The term "Information sharing" in the information technology lexicon has a long history.

Privacy	Privacy has no definite boundaries and it has different meanings for different people. It is the ability of an individual or group to keep their lives and personal affairs out of public view, or to control the flow of information about themselves.
Security	Security is the condition of being protected against danger or loss.
Social	Social refers to human society or its organization. Although the term is a crucial category in social science and often used in public discourse, its meaning is at times vague, suggesting that it is a fuzzy concept. An added difficulty is that social attributes or relationships may not be directly observable and visible, and must be inferred by abstract thought.
Social Security	Social security primarily refers to social welfare service concerned with social protection, or protection against socially recognized conditions, including poverty, old age, disability, unemployment and others.
Addiction	A pattern of behavior characterized by an overwhelming involvement with using a drug and securing its supply is defined as an addiction.
Alcohol abuse	Alcohol abuse, as described in the DSM-IV, is a psychiatric diagnosis describing the use of alcoholic beverages despite negative consequences.
Domestic violence	Domestic violence occurs when a family member, partner or ex-partner attempts to physically or psychologically dominate another. Domestic violence often refers to violence between spouses, or spousal abuse but can also include cohabitants and non-married intimate partners. Domestic violence occurs in all cultures; people of all races, ethnicities, religions, sexes and classes can be perpetrators of domestic violence. Domestic violence is perpetrated by both men and women.
Homelessness	Homelessness is the condition and societal category of people who lack housing and food, usually because they cannot afford a regular, safe, and adequate shelter. The term "homelessness" may also include people whose primary nighttime residence is in a homeless shelter, in an institution that provides a temporary residence for individuals intended to be institutionalized, or in a public or private place not designed for use as a regular sleeping accommodation for human beings.
Mental health	Mental health is a term used to describe either a level of cognitive or emotional wellbeing or an absence of a mental disorder.
Behavior	Behavior refers to the actions or reactions of an object or organism, usually in relation to the environment. Humans evaluate the acceptability of behavior using social norms and regulate behavior by means of social control. In sociology, behavior is considered as having no meaning, being not directed at other people and thus is the most basic human action.

Child abuse	Child abuse is the physical, sexual, or emotional maltreatment or neglect of children by parents, guardians, or others. Child abuse in its various forms has numerous effects and consequences, both tangible and intangible, upon society, those mistreated, and those entrusted with the responsibility of its detection, prevention and treatment.
Employment	Employment is a contract between two parties, one being the employer and the other being the employee. An employee may be defined as: "A person in the service of another under any contract of hire, express or implied, oral or written, where the employer has the power or right to control and direct the employee in the material details of how the work is to be performed."
Family reunification	Family reunification is a recognized reason for immigration in many countries. The presence of one or more family members in a certain country, therefore, enables the rest of the family to immigrate to that country as well. family reunification laws try to balance the right of a family to live together, or the right of a person to marry whomever he chooses, with the country"s right to control immigration.
Sacred Contagion	Sacred Contagion is the belief that spiritual properties within an object, place place usually by direct contact or physical proximity. While the concept of Sacred Contagion has existed in numerous cultures since before recorded history, the term "Sacred Contagion" originated with French sociologist Émile Durkheim, who introduced it in his book The Elementary Forms of Religious Life. An example of Sacred Contagion is chapters 11 through 15 in the Book of Leviticus found in the Bible and Torah.
Personal Responsibility and Work Opportunity Reconciliation Act	The Personal Responsibility and Work Opportunity Reconciliation Act of 1996 is a United States federal law considered to be a fundamental shift in both the method and goal of federal cash assistance to the poor.
State government	A state government is the government of a subnational entity in states with federal forms of government, which shares political power with the federal government or national government. A state government may have some level of political autonomy, or be subject to the direct control of the federal government.
Adolescence	Adolescence (lat adolescere, (to grow) is a transitional stage of physical and mental human development that occurs between childhood and adulthood. This transition involves biological (i.e. pubertal), social, and psychological changes, though the biological or physiological ones are the easiest to measure objectively. Historically, puberty has been heavily associated with teenagers and the onset of adolescent development.[1][2] In recent years, however, the start of puberty has had somewhat of an increase in preAdolescence (particularly females), and Adolescence has had an occasional extension beyond the teenage years (typically males).
Emancipation	Emancipation is a term used to describe various efforts to obtain political rights or equality, often for a specifically disenfranchised group, or more generally in discussion of such matters.

Minor	In law, the term minor is used to refer to a person who is under the age in which one legally assumes adulthood and is legally granted rights afforded to adults in society. Depending on the jurisdiction and application, this age may vary, but is usually marked at either 18 or 21. Specifically, the status of "minor" is defined by the age of majority[
Teenage pregnancy	Teenage pregnancy is defined as an underaged girl becoming pregnant with a baby. While women technically stay in their "teens" until the age of 20, the term is restricted to those under the age threshold of legal adulthood, which is 18 in most of the United States, and 16 in much of the rest of the world.
Pregnancy	Pregnancy is the carrying of one or more offspring, known as a fetus or embryo, inside the body of a female mammal such as a human, between conception and birth. In many societies" medical and legal definitions, human pregnancy is somewhat arbitrarily divided into three trimester periods, as a means to simplify reference to the different stages of prenatal development.
Delinquent	Delinquent means one who fails to do that which is required by law or by duty when such failure is minor in nature.
Attachment	In attachment theory psychology, attachment is a product of the activity of a number of behavioral systems that have proximity to a person, e.g. a mother, as a predictable outcome. The concept of there being an "attachment" behavior, stage, and process, to which a growing person remains in proximity to another was developed beginning in 1956 by British developmental psychologist John Bowlby.
Post traumatic stress disorder	Post traumatic stress disorder is an anxiety disorder that can develop after exposure to one or more terrifying events in which grave physical harm occurred or was threatened.
Safety	Safety is the state of being "safe", the condition of being protected against physical, social, spiritual, financial, political, emotional, occupational, psychological, educational or other types or consequences of failure, damage, error, accidents, harm or any other event which could be considered non-desirable.
Stress	Stress is the consequence of the failure to adapt to change. Less simply: it is the condition that results when person-environment transactions lead the individual to perceive a discrepancy, whether real or not, between the demands of a situation and the resources of the person"s biological, psychological or social systems.
Quality of life	The quality of life of a population is an important concern in economics and political science. It is measured by many social and economic factors. A large part is standard of living, the amount of money and access to goods and services that a person has; these numbers are fairly easily measured.

Education	Education encompasses teaching and learning specific skills, and also something less tangible but more profound: the imparting of knowledge, positive judgement and well-developed wisdom. Education has as one of its fundamental aspects the imparting of culture from generation to generation.
Need	A Need is something that is necessary for humans to live a healthy life. Need s are distinguished from wants because a deficiency would cause a clear negative outcome, such as dysfunction or death. Need s can be objective and physical, such as food and water, or they can be subjective and psychological, such as the Need for self-esteem.
From each according to his ability, to each according to his need	From each according to his ability, to each according to his need is a slogan popularized by Karl Marx in his 1875 Critique of the Gotha Program. The phrase summarizes the principles that, under a communist system, every person should contribute to society to the best of his ability and consume from society in proportion to his needs, regardless of how much he has contributed. In the Marxist view, such an arrangement will be made possible by the abundance of goods and services that a developed communist society will produce; the idea is that there will be enough to satisfy everyone"s needs.
Group therapy	Group therapy is a form of psychotherapy during which one or several therapists treat a small group of clients together as a group. This may be more cost effective than individual therapy, and possibly even more productive.
Sibling	A Sibling is a brother or a sister; that is, any person who shares at least one of the same parents. In most societies throughout the world, Sibling s usually grow up together and spend a good deal of their childhood with each other. This genetic and physical closeness may be marked by the development of strong emotional associations such as love or enmity.
Groups	In sociology, a group can be defined as two or more humans that interact with one another, accept expectations and obligations as members of the group, and share a common identity. By this definition, society can be viewed as a large group, though most social groups are considerably smaller.
Gay	Gay usually describes a person"s sexual orientation, being the standard term for homosexual. Gay sometimes also refers to commonalities shared by homosexual people, as in "gay history", the ideological concept of a hypothetical gay culture, as in "gay music." The word gay is sometimes used to refer to same-sex relationships.
Lesbian	A lesbian is a woman who is romantically and sexually attracted only to other women. Some women in same-sex relationships do not identify as lesbian, but as bisexual, queer, or another label. As with any interpersonal activity, sexual expression depends on the context of the relationship.
Youth	Youth is defined by as, "The time of life when one is young; especially: a: the period between childhood and maturity b: the early period of existence, growth, or development."

Independence	Independence is the self-government of a nation, country, or state by its residents and population, or some portion thereof, generally exercising sovereignty.
Committed relationship	A committed relationship is an interpersonal relationship based upon a mutually agreed upon pledge to one another involving exclusivity, honesty, or some other agreed upon behavior.
Trend	A trend is something that somehow becomes popular within mainstream society over a long period of time. It is the direction of a sequence of events that has some momentum and durability.
Who	The World Health Organization is a specialized agency of the United Nations that acts as a coordinating authority on international public health. Established on 7 April 1948, and headquartered in Geneva, Switzerland, the agency inherited the mandate and resources of its predecessor, the Health Organization, which had been an agency of the League of Nations. The WHO"s constitution states that its objective "is the attainment by all peoples of the highest possible level of health." Its major task is to combat disease, especially key infectious diseases, and to promote the general health of the people of the world.
Substance Abuse	Substance abuse refers to the overindulgence in and dependence on a psychoactive leading to effects that are detrimental to the individual"s physical health or mental health, or the welfare of others.
Website	A website (or web site) is a collection of related web pages, images, videos or other digital assets that are addressed with a common domain name or IP address in an Internet Protocol-based network. A web site is hosted on at least one web server, accessible via the Internet or a private local area network. A web page is a document, typically written in plain text interspersed with formatting instructions of Hypertext Markup Language (HTML, XHTML.)
Association	Association in archaeology has more than one meaning and is confusing to the layman. Archaeology has been critiqued as a soft science with a somewhat poor standardization of terms. Associated finds or objects refers to a close relationship between two or more objects.
Resource	A resource is any physical or virtual entity of limited availability, or anything used to help one earn a living. In most cases, commercial or even ethic factors require resource allocation through resource management. As resource s are very useful, we attach some information value to them.
Title IV	Title IV of the Higher Education Act of 1965 (the Act, the HSA) covers the administration of the United States federal student financial aid programs. American colleges and universities are generally classified with regard to their inclusion under Title IV, such as under the U.S. Department of Education statistics .

Adoption	Adoption is the legal act of permanently placing a child with a parent or parents other than the birth mother or father. An adoption order has the effect of severing the parental responsibilities and rights of the birth parents and transferring those responsibilities and rights onto the adoptive parents.
African Americans	African Americans are citizens or residents of the United States whose ancestors, usually in predominant part, were indigenous to Sub-Saharan Africa. Most are the descendants of captive Africans who were enslaved within the boundaries of the present United States.
Father	The father is defined as the male parent of an offspring. The adjective "paternal" refers to father, parallel to "maternal" for mother. According to the anthropologist Maurice Godelier, the parental role assumed by human males is a critical difference between human society and that of humans" closest biological relatives - chimpanzees and bonobos - who appear to be unaware of their "father" connection.
Adolescence	Adolescence (lat adolescere, (to grow) is a transitional stage of physical and mental human development that occurs between childhood and adulthood. This transition involves biological (i.e. pubertal), social, and psychological changes, though the biological or physiological ones are the easiest to measure objectively. Historically, puberty has been heavily associated with teenagers and the onset of adolescent development.[1][2] In recent years, however, the start of puberty has had somewhat of an increase in preAdolescence (particularly females), and Adolescence has had an occasional extension beyond the teenage years (typically males).
Infant	In basic English usage, an infant is defined as a human child at the youngest stage of life, specifically before they can walk and generally before the age of one.
International adoption	International adoption is a type of adoption in which an individual or couple becomes the legal and permanent parents of a child born in another country. In general, prospective adoptive parents must meet the legal adoption requirements of their country of residence and those of the country in which the child was born.
Minor	In law, the term minor is used to refer to a person who is under the age in which one legally assumes adulthood and is legally granted rights afforded to adults in society. Depending on the jurisdiction and application, this age may vary, but is usually marked at either 18 or 21. Specifically, the status of "minor" is defined by the age of majority[
Mother	A mother is a biological and/or social female parent of an offspring. In the case of a mammal such as a human, the biological mother gestates a fertilized ovum, which is called first an embryo, and then a fetus. This gestation occurs in the mother"s uterus from conception until the fetus is sufficiently developed to be born. The mother then goes into labor and gives birth. Once the child is born, the mother produces milk in a process called lactation to feed the child; often the mother"s breast milk is the child"s sole nourishment for the first year or more of the child"s life.

Native Americans	Native Americans in the United States are the indigenous peoples from the regions of North America now encompassed by the continental United States, including parts of Alaska. They comprise a large number of distinct tribes, states, and ethnic groups, many of which are still enduring as political communities.
State government	A state government is the government of a subnational entity in states with federal forms of government, which shares political power with the federal government or national government. A state government may have some level of political autonomy, or be subject to the direct control of the federal government.
Teenage pregnancy	Teenage pregnancy is defined as an underaged girl becoming pregnant with a baby. While women technically stay in their "teens" until the age of 20, the term is restricted to those under the age threshold of legal adulthood, which is 18 in most of the United States, and 16 in much of the rest of the world.
Pregnancy	Pregnancy is the carrying of one or more offspring, known as a fetus or embryo, inside the body of a female mammal such as a human, between conception and birth. In many societies" medical and legal definitions, human pregnancy is somewhat arbitrarily divided into three trimester periods, as a means to simplify reference to the different stages of prenatal development.
Child	A child is a boy or girl who has not reached puberty, but also refers to offspring of any age.
Delinquent	Delinquent means one who fails to do that which is required by law or by duty when such failure is minor in nature.
Experience	Experience as a general concept comprises knowledge of or skill in or observation of some thing or some event gained through involvement in or exposure to that thing or event. The history of the word experience aligns it closely with the concept of experiment.
Right	In jurisprudence and law, a right is the legal or moral entitlement to do or refrain from doing something or to obtain or refrain from obtaining an action, thing or recognition in civil society. Compare with privilege, or a thing to which one has a just claim. They serve as rules of interaction between people, and, as such, they place constraints and obligations upon the actions of individuals or groups.
Triad	Triad, a general term for criminal organizations, is a collective term that describes many branches of an underground society and organizations based in Hong Kong and also operating in Macau, Taiwan, mainland China, and countries with significant Chinese populations such as Malaysia, Singapore and also Chinatowns in Europe, North America, South Africa, Australia and New Zealand.

197

Confidentiality	Confidentiality has been defined by the International Organization for Standardization as "ensuring that information is accessible only to those authorized to have access" and is one of the cornerstones of Information security. Confidentiality is one of the design goals for many cryptosystems, made possible in practice by the techniques of modern cryptography.
White people	White people is a term which is usually used to refer to human beings characterized, at least in part, by the light pigmentation of their skin. It often refers narrowly to people claiming ancestry exclusively from Europe. A broadly corresponding concept was the Caucasian race.
Historical	((race)) The historical definition of race was an immutable and distinct type or species, sharing distinct racial characteristics such as constitution, temperament, and mental abilities.
	These races were not conceived as being related with each other, but formed a hierarchy of inherent value called the Great Chain of Being with Europeans usually at the top. As time progressed, Charles Darwin"s theory of evolution was applied to races.
Abortion	An abortion is the removal or expulsion of an embryo or fetus from the uterus, resulting in or caused by its death. This can occur spontaneously as a miscarriage or be artificially induced by chemical, surgical or other means.
Underground economy	The underground economy consists of all commerce on which applicable taxes are being evaded. The market includes not only legally-prohibited commerce, but also trade in legal goods and services because some income is not reported and consequently taxation is evaded, e.g., through money laundering, payment in cash, or other means.
Family	A family consists of a domestic group of people, typically affiliated by birth or marriage, or by analogous or comparable relationships — including domestic partnership, cohabitation, adoption, surname and ownership.
Single-parent	A Single-parent is a parent who cares for children without the assistance of another person in the home. The legal definition of "single parenthood" may vary according to the local laws of different nations or regions.
Single parent	A single parent is a parent who cares for one or more children without the assistance of another parent in the home. The legal definition may vary according to the local laws of different nations or regions.
Child Protective Services	Child Protective Services is the name of a governmental agency in many states in the United States that responds to allegations of child abuse or neglect.
Open adoption	A system of adoption in which the birth mother is permitted to meet and play an active role in selecting the adoptive parents and to maintain some form of contact with her child depending on the agreement reached is referred to as an open adoption.

Welfare reform	Welfare reform is the name for a policy change in countries with a state-administered social welfare system to reduce dependence on welfare, as demanded by political conservatives. A movement to change the federal government"s social welfare policy which shifted responsibility to the states and cut benefits.
Welfare	Welfare is financial assistance paid by taxpayers to people who are unable to support themselves. Some welfare is general, while specific and can only be invoked under certain circumstances, such as a scholarship. Individuals may apply for welfare due to disability, lack of education or job training, a low demand for unskilled labor, substance abuse, or an unwillingness to work.
Analysis	Analysis is the process of breaking a complex topic or substance into smaller parts to gain a better understanding of it. The technique has been applied in the study of mathematics and logic since before Aristotle, though analysis as a formal concept is a relatively recent development. As a formal concept, the method has variously been ascribed by Ibn al-Haytham, Descartes, Galileo, and Isaac Newton, as a practical method of physical discovery.
Federal government	A federal government is the common government of a federation. The structure of federal government s vary from institution to institution based on a broad definition of a basic federal political system, there are two or more levels of government that exist within an established territory and govern through common institutions with overlapping or shared powers as prescribed by a constitution. · Government of Australia · Government of Belgium · Government of Brazil · Government of Canada · Government of Germany · Government of India · Government of Malaysia · Government of Mexico · Government of Russia · Government of Switzerland · Government of the United States The United States is considered the first modern federation. After declaring independence from Britain, the U.S. adopted its first constitution, the Articles of Confederation in 1781.
Foster Care	Foster care is a system by which a certified, stand-in "parent" cares for minor children or young peoples who have been removed from their birth parents or other custodial adults by state authority. Responsibility for the young person is assumed by the relevant governmental authority and a placement with another family found. There can be voluntary placements by a parent of a child into foster care.
Government	A government is a body that has the authority to make and the power to enforce laws within a civil, corporate, religious, academic, or other organization or group.

Internet	The Internet is a global system of interconnected computer networks that interchange data by packet switching using the standardized Internet Protocol Suite. It is a "network of networks" that consists of millions of private and public, academic, business, and government networks of local to global scope that are linked by copper wires, fiber-optic cables, wireless connections, and other technologies. The Internet carries various information resources and services, such as electronic mail, online chat, file transfer and file sharing, online gaming, and the inter-linked hypertext documents and other resources of the World Wide Web.
Questionnaire	A questionnaire is a research instrument consisting of a series of questions and other prompts for the purpose of gathering information from respondents. Although they are often designed for statistical analysis of the responses, this is not always the case.
Kinship	Kinship is a relationship between any entities that share a genealogical origin, through either biological, cultural, or historical descent. In anthropology the kinship system includes people related both by descent and marriage, while usage in biology includes descent and mating. Human kinship relations through marriage are commonly called "affinity" in contrast to "descent" also called "consanguinity", although the two may overlap in marriages among those of common descent. Family relations as sociocultural genealogy lead back to gods
Pattern	A pattern, from the French patron, is a type of theme of recurring events of or objects, sometimes referred to as elements of a set. These elements repeat in a predictable manner. It can be a template or model which can be used to generate things or parts of a thing, especially if the things that are created have enough in common for the underlying pattern to be inferred, in which case the things are said to exhibit the unique pattern.
Agency	Agency is an area of commercial law dealing with a contractual or quasi-contractual tripartite, or non-contractual set of relationships when an Agent is authorized to act on behalf of another to create a legal relationship with a Third Party. Succinctly, it may be referred to as the relationship between a principal and an agent whereby the principal, expressly or impliedly, authorizes the agent to work under his control and on his behalf. The agent is, thus, required to negotiate on behalf of the principal or bring him and third parties into contractual relationship.
Counseling	Counseling can be defined as a relatively short-term, interpersonal, theory-based process of helping persons who are fundamentally psychologically healthy resolve developmental and situational issues.
Adoption and Safe Families Act	The Adoption and Safe Families Act was signed into law by President Bill Clinton on November 19, 1997 after having been approved by the United States Congress earlier in the month. It was enacted in an attempt to correct problems that were inherent in the foster care system that deterred the adoption of children with special needs.
Lesbian	A lesbian is a woman who is romantically and sexually attracted only to other women. Some women in same-sex relationships do not identify as lesbian, but as bisexual, queer, or another label. As with any interpersonal activity, sexual expression depends on the context of the relationship.

Book	A book is a set or collection of written, printed, illustrated made of paper, parchment usually fastened together to hinge at one side. A single sheet within a book is called a leaf, and each side of a leaf is called a page. A book produced in electronic format is known as an e-book.
Court	A court is a public forum used by a power base to adjudicate disputes and dispense civil, labor, administrative and criminal justice under its laws. In common law and civil law states, courts are the central means for dispute resolution, and it is generally understood that all persons have an ability to bring their claims before a court. Similarly, those accused of a crime have the right to present their defense before a court.
International law	International law can refer to three distinct legal disciplines. Public international law which involves for instance the United Nations, maritime law, international criminal law and the Geneva conventions. Private international law or conflict of laws, which addresses the question of which legal jurisdiction cases may be heard in. Last, supranational law, which concerns at present regional agreements where the special distinguishing quality.
Legal systems of the world	The three major legal systems of the world today consist of civil law, common law and religious law. However, each country often develops variations on each system or incorporates many other features into the system.
Resource	A resource is any physical or virtual entity of limited availability, or anything used to help one earn a living. In most cases, commercial or even ethic factors require resource allocation through resource management. As resource s are very useful, we attach some information value to them.
Court of last resort	In some countries, provinces and states, the court of last resort is the highest court whose rulings cannot be challenged.
Abandonment	Parents that physically leave their children with the intention of completely severing the parent-child relationship are engaging in abandonment.To give up control of a child, legally terminating parental rights; in many states abandonment is considered child abuse.
Abuse	Abuse refers to the use or treatment of something that is seen as harmful. The term can be used for anything ranging from the misuse of a piece of equipment to the severe maltreatment of a person.
Contact	In Family Law, contact is one of the general terms which denotes the level of contact a parent or other significant person in a child"s life can have with that child. Contact forms part of the bundle of rights and privileges which a parent may have in relation to any child of the family.
Attachment	In attachment theory psychology, attachment is a product of the activity of a number of behavioral systems that have proximity to a person, e.g. a mother, as a predictable outcome. The concept of there being an "attachment" behavior, stage, and process, to which a growing person remains in proximity to another was developed beginning in 1956 by British developmental psychologist John Bowlby.

Cooperative	A cooperative is an autonomous association of persons united voluntarily to meet their common economic, social, and cultural needs and aspirations through a jointly-owned and democratically-controlled enterprise.
Crisis	A crisis may occur on a personal or societal level. It may be a traumatic or stressful change in a person"s life, or an unstable and dangerous social situation, in political, social, economic, military affairs, or a large-scale environmental event, especially one involving an impending abrupt change. More loosely, it is a term meaning "a testing time" or "emergency event".
Behavior	Behavior refers to the actions or reactions of an object or organism, usually in relation to the environment. Humans evaluate the acceptability of behavior using social norms and regulate behavior by means of social control. In sociology, behavior is considered as having no meaning, being not directed at other people and thus is the most basic human action.
Groups	In sociology, a group can be defined as two or more humans that interact with one another, accept expectations and obligations as members of the group, and share a common identity. By this definition, society can be viewed as a large group, though most social groups are considerably smaller.
Adult	The term adult describes any mature organism, but normally it refers to a human: one that is no longer a child / minor and is now either a man or a woman. It can be defined in terms of biology, law, personal character, or social status. These different aspects are often inconsistent and contradictory.
Sexual abuse	Sexual abuse is defined by the forcing of undesired sexual acts by one person to another.
Cultural competence	Cultural competence refers to an ability to interact effectively with people of different cultures.
Planning	Planning in organizations and public policy is both the organizational process of creating and maintaining a plan; and the psychological process of thinking about the activities required to create a desired future on some scale.
Mean	In statistics, Mean has two related Mean ings: · the arithmetic Mean · the expected value of a random variable, which is also called the population Mean It is sometimes stated that the Mean Mean s average. This is incorrect if Mean is taken in the specific sense of "arithmetic Mean as there are different types of averages: the Mean median, and mode. Other simple statistical analyses use measures of spread, such as range, interquartile range, or standard deviation. For a real-valued random variable X, the Mean is the expectation of X. Note that not every probability distribution has a defined Mean (or variance); see the Cauchy distribution for an example.

Women	A woman is a female human. The term woman irregular plural: women usually is used for an adult, with the term girl being the usual term for a female child or adolescent. However, the term woman is also sometimes used to identify a female human, regardless of age, as in phrases such as "Women"s rights".
Interest	Interest is a fee paid on borrowed assets. By far the most common form these assets are lent in is money, but other assets may be lent to the borrower, such as shares, consumer goods through hire purchase, major assets such as aircraft, and even entire factories in finance lease arrangements. In each case the interest is calculated upon the value of the assets in the same manner as upon money.
Workforce	The workforce is the labor pool in employment. It is generally used to describe those working for a single company or industry. The term generally excludes the employers or management, and implies those involved in manual labor. It may also mean all those that are available for work.
Extended family	Extended family refers to a family group consisting of more than two generations of the same kinship line living either within the same household or, more usually in the west, very close to one another.
Family preservation	Family preservation was the movement to help keep children at home with their families rather than in foster homes or institutions. This movement was a reaction to the earlier policy of family breakup, which pulled children out of unfit homes. Extreme poverty alone was seen as a justified reason to remove children.
Association	Association in archaeology has more than one meaning and is confusing to the layman. Archaeology has been critiqued as a soft science with a somewhat poor standardization of terms. Associated finds or objects refers to a close relationship between two or more objects.
Slavery	Slavery refers to an extreme form of stratification in which some people are owned by others.
Social	Social refers to human society or its organization. Although the term is a crucial category in social science and often used in public discourse, its meaning is at times vague, suggesting that it is a fuzzy concept. An added difficulty is that social attributes or relationships may not be directly observable and visible, and must be inferred by abstract thought.
Boarding school	A boarding school is a school where some or all pupils not only study, but also live during term time, with their fellow students and possibly teachers.
Bureau of Indian Affairs	The Bureau of Indian Affairs is an agency of the federal government of the United States within the Department of the Interior charged with the administration and management of 55.7 million acres of land held in trust by the United States for American Indians, Indian tribes and Alaska Natives. In addition, the Bureau of Indian Affairs provides education services to approximately 48,000 Indians.
Committee	A committee is a type of small deliberative assembly that is usually subordinate to another, larger deliberative assembly.

Culture	Culture generally refers to patterns of human activity and the symbolic structures that give such activity significant importance. Culture has been called "the way of life for an entire society." As such, it includes codes of manners, dress, language, religion, rituals, norms of behavior such as law and morality, and systems of belief.
Hispanic	Hispanic is a term that historically denoted relation to the ancient Hispania and its peoples. The term now refers to the culture and people of the Spanish-speaking countries of Hispanic America and Spain; or countries with a historical legacy from Spain, including the Southwestern United States and Florida; the African nations of Equatorial Guinea, Western Sahara and the Northern coastal region of Morocco; the Asia-Pacific nations of the Philippines, Guam, Northern Mariana Islands; and to the ethnic individuals of those cultures. It can also refer to the Hispanosphere geographical distribution, the same way Latin refers to the Romance languages in general.
Latino	Latino is a term that is historically denoted relation to the ancient Latina tribe, who were an ancient Italic people who migrated to central Italy. Since its official adoption, the definition and usage of the term by the Federal Government is strictly as an ethnic, as opposed to racial, identifier, used together with the term Hispanic.
Ethnicity	Ethnicity is a population of human beings whose members identify with each other, either on the basis of a presumed common genealogy or ancestry or recognition by others as a distinct group, or by common cultural, linguistic, religious, or physical traits. The sociologist Max Weber once remarked that "The whole conception of it is so complex and so vague that it might be good to abandon it altogether."
Hurricane	A hurricane is one of many meteorological terms for a storm system characterized by a low pressure center and thunderstorms that produces strong wind and flooding rain. It feeds on the heat released when moist air rises and the water vapor it contains condenses.
Hurricane Katrina	Hurricane Katrina was the costliest and one of the five deadliest hurricanes in the history of the United States. It was the sixth-strongest Atlantic hurricane ever recorded and the third-strongest hurricane on record that made landfall in the United States. Katrina formed on August 23 during the 2005 Atlantic hurricane season and caused devastation along much of the north-central Gulf Coast. The most severe loss of life and property damage occurred in New Orleans, Louisiana, which flooded as the levee system catastrophically failed, in many cases hours after the storm had moved inland.
Pacific Islander	Pacific Islander is a geographic term to describe the inhabitants of any of the three major sub-regions of Oceania: Polynesia, Melanesia and Micronesia. According to the Encyclopaedia Britannica, these three regions, together with their islands consist of:
Child abuse	Child abuse is the physical, sexual, or emotional maltreatment or neglect of children by parents, guardians, or others. Child abuse in its various forms has numerous effects and consequences, both tangible and intangible, upon society, those mistreated, and those entrusted with the responsibility of its detection, prevention and treatment.
Origin	Origins can refer to:

· Origins Game Fair, a gaming convention
· Origins Award, presented by the Academy of Adventure Gaming Arts and Design
· Origins, a plant-based skin care and fragrance company of Estée Lauder
· Origins, a Nova mini-series about the origin of life and the origin of the universe
· Origins Institute, a department at McMaster University
· Origins, a fantasy novel in the Fourth World series by Kate Thompson

· "Origins", a major Judge Dredd storyline running from 2006 through 2007
· Secret Files and Origins and Secret Origins, two comic book series published by DC Comics that told the origins of different characters
· Wolverine: Origins, a Marvel Comics series, the sequel to Wolverine: Origin

· Origins, the fourth mainstream studio album by Safri Duo .

Race	The term race refers to the concept of dividing people into populations or groups on the basis of various sets of characteristics and beliefs about common ancestry. The most widely used human racial categories are based on visible traits especially skin color, facial features and hair texture, and self-identification.
Social Work	Social work is a helping profession focused on social change, problem solving in human relationships and the empowerment and liberation of people to enhance well-being.
China	China is a cultural region, ancient civilization, and nation in East Asia. It is one of the world"s oldest civilizations, consisting of states and cultures dating back more than six millennia. The stalemate of the last Chinese Civil War has resulted in two political entities using the name: the People"s Republic of China, administering mainland China, Hong Kong, and Macau; and the Republic of China, administering Taiwan and its surrounding islands.
Convention	A convention is a set of agreed, stipulated or generally accepted social norms, norms, standards or criteria, often taking the form of a custom.
Hague Convention	The longtime status of the Netherlands as a largely neutral nation in international conflicts and the corresponding ascendance of The Hague as a primary location for diplomatic and international conferences has led to several negotiated conventions over the years being termed the Hague Convention.
Citizenship	Citizenship is membership in a society, community, or and carries with it rights to political participation; a person having such membership is a citizen.

Evidence-based practice	The term evidence-based practice refers to preferential use of mental and behavioral health interventions for which systematic empirical research has provided evidence of statistically significant effectiveness as treatments for specific problems. It is an approach which tries to specify the way in which professionals or other decision-makers should make decisions by identifying such evidence that there may be for a practice, and rating it according to how scientifically sound it may be. Its goal is to eliminate unsound or excessively risky practices in favour of those that have better outcomes.
Cost	In economics, business, and accounting, a cost is the value of money that has been used up to produce something, and hence is not available for use anymore.
American Academy of Pediatrics	The American Academy of Pediatrics is an organization of pediatricians, physicians trained to deal with the medical care of infants, children, and adolescents. It is a partner in the Campaign for Children"s Health Care, a multi-year campaign to raise awareness about the problem of uninsured children in America.
Gay	Gay usually describes a person"s sexual orientation, being the standard term for homosexual. Gay sometimes also refers to commonalities shared by homosexual people, as in "gay history", the ideological concept of a hypothetical gay culture, as in "gay music." The word gay is sometimes used to refer to same-sex relationships.
Sibling	A Sibling is a brother or a sister; that is, any person who shares at least one of the same parents. In most societies throughout the world, Sibling s usually grow up together and spend a good deal of their childhood with each other. This genetic and physical closeness may be marked by the development of strong emotional associations such as love or enmity.
Data Analysis	Qualitative data analysis QDA or qualitative research is the analysis of non-numerical data, for example words, photographs, observations, etc..
Policy	A policy is a deliberate plan of action to guide decisions and achieve rational outcomes. The term may apply to government, private sector organizations and groups, and individuals. Presidential executive orders, corporate privacy policies, and parliamentary rules of order are all examples of policy. Policy differs from rules or law. While law can compel or prohibit behaviors policy merely guides actions toward those that are most likely to achieve a desired outcome.
Website	A website (or web site) is a collection of related web pages, images, videos or other digital assets that are addressed with a common domain name or IP address in an Internet Protocol-based network. A web site is hosted on at least one web server, accessible via the Internet or a private local area network. A web page is a document, typically written in plain text interspersed with formatting instructions of Hypertext Markup Language (HTML, XHTML.)

Minor	In law, the term minor is used to refer to a person who is under the age in which one legally assumes adulthood and is legally granted rights afforded to adults in society. Depending on the jurisdiction and application, this age may vary, but is usually marked at either 18 or 21. Specifically, the status of "minor" is defined by the age of majority[
Delinquent	Delinquent means one who fails to do that which is required by law or by duty when such failure is minor in nature.
Adult	The term adult describes any mature organism, but normally it refers to a human: one that is no longer a child / minor and is now either a man or a woman. It can be defined in terms of biology, law, personal character, or social status. These different aspects are often inconsistent and contradictory.
Hurricane	A hurricane is one of many meteorological terms for a storm system characterized by a low pressure center and thunderstorms that produces strong wind and flooding rain. It feeds on the heat released when moist air rises and the water vapor it contains condenses.
Hurricane Katrina	Hurricane Katrina was the costliest and one of the five deadliest hurricanes in the history of the United States. It was the sixth-strongest Atlantic hurricane ever recorded and the third-strongest hurricane on record that made landfall in the United States. Katrina formed on August 23 during the 2005 Atlantic hurricane season and caused devastation along much of the north-central Gulf Coast. The most severe loss of life and property damage occurred in New Orleans, Louisiana, which flooded as the levee system catastrophically failed, in many cases hours after the storm had moved inland.
Internet	The Internet is a global system of interconnected computer networks that interchange data by packet switching using the standardized Internet Protocol Suite. It is a "network of networks" that consists of millions of private and public, academic, business, and government networks of local to global scope that are linked by copper wires, fiber-optic cables, wireless connections, and other technologies. The Internet carries various information resources and services, such as electronic mail, online chat, file transfer and file sharing, online gaming, and the inter-linked hypertext documents and other resources of the World Wide Web.
Violence	*Violence* is the exertion of force with the intent to injure (psychologically or physically) or kill. *Violence* is also used more broadly and metaphorically to describe the destructive action of natural phenomena like storms and earthquakes. Variant uses of the term refer to the destruction of non-living objects
Violent crime	A Violent crime or crime of violence is a crime in which the offender uses or threatens to use violent force upon the victim. This entails both crimes in which the violent act is the objective, such as murder, as well as crimes in which violence is the means to an end, such as robbery. Violent crime s include crimes committed with and without weapons.
White people	White people is a term which is usually used to refer to human beings characterized, at least in part, by the light pigmentation of their skin. It often refers narrowly to people claiming ancestry exclusively from Europe. A broadly corresponding concept was the Caucasian race.

Adoption	Adoption is the legal act of permanently placing a child with a parent or parents other than the birth mother or father. An adoption order has the effect of severing the parental responsibilities and rights of the birth parents and transferring those responsibilities and rights onto the adoptive parents.
Juvenile delinquency	Juvenile delinquency refers to criminal acts performed by juveniles. It may refer to either violent or non-violent crime committed by persons who are under the age of eighteen and are still considered to be a minor. There is much debate about whether or not such a child should be held criminally responsible for his or her own actions.
Time	Time is a component of a measuring system used to sequence events, to compare the durations of events and the intervals between them, and to quantify the motions of objects. Time has been a major subject of religion, philosophy, and science, but defining time in a non-controversial manner applicable to all fields of study has consistently eluded the greatest scholars. In physics and other sciences, time is considered one of the few fundamental quantities.
Curfew	A curfew can be one of the following; an order by a government for certain persons to return home daily before a certain time, an order by the legal guardians of a minor to return home by a specific time, usually in the evening or night, or a daily requirement for guests to return to their hostel before a specified time, usually in the evening or night.
Status	In sociology or anthropology, social status is the honor or prestige attached to one"s position in society one"s social position. The stratification system, which is the system of distributing rewards to the members of society, determines social status. Social status, the position or rank of a person or group within the stratification system, can be determined two ways. One can earn their social status by their own achievements, which is known as achieved status, or one can be placed in the stratification system by their inherited position, which is called ascribed status.
Truancy	Truancy is a term used to describe any intentional unauthorized absence from compulsory schooling.
Court	A court is a public forum used by a power base to adjudicate disputes and dispense civil, labor, administrative and criminal justice under its laws. In common law and civil law states, courts are the central means for dispute resolution, and it is generally understood that all persons have an ability to bring their claims before a court. Similarly, those accused of a crime have the right to present their defense before a court.
Scope	In a sociological context, a scope is the state of an environment in which a situation exists. It is defined as a public place or institution where society has universally agreed that certain behaviors are considered to be acceptable while others are not.
Behavior	Behavior refers to the actions or reactions of an object or organism, usually in relation to the environment. Humans evaluate the acceptability of behavior using social norms and regulate behavior by means of social control. In sociology, behavior is considered as having no meaning, being not directed at other people and thus is the most basic human action.

Homicide	Homicide refers to the act of killing another human being. It can also describe a person who has committed such an act, though this use is rare in modern English. Although homicide does not define an illegal act necessarily, sometimes it is used synonymously with "murder."
Risk	Risk is a concept that denotes the precise probability of specific eventualities. Technically, the notion of Risk is independent from the notion of value and, as such, eventualities may have both beneficial and adverse consequences. However, in general usage the convention is to focus only on potential negative impact to some characteristic of value that may arise from a future event.
Youth	Youth is defined by as, "The time of life when one is young; especially: a: the period between childhood and maturity b: the early period of existence, growth, or development."
Youth Risk Behavior Survey	The Youth Risk Behavior Survey is an American biannual survey of adolescent health risk and health protective behaviors such as smoking, drinking, drug use, diet, and physical activity conducted by the Centers for Disease Control and Prevention. It is one of the major sources of information about these risk behaviors, and is used by federal agencies to track drug use, sexual behavior, and other risk behaviors. The Youth Risk Behavior Survey was created in the early 1990s in order to monitor progress towards protecting youth from HIV infection.
Arrest	An arrest is the act of depriving a person of his or her liberty usually in relation to the investigation and prevention of crime. The term is Norman in origin and is related to the French word arrêt, meaning "stop".
Crime rate	Crime rate is a measure of the rate of occurrence of crimes committed in a given area and time. Most commonly, crime rate is given as the number of crimes committed among a given number of persons.
New York	New York is a state in the Mid-Atlantic and Northeastern regions of the United States of America. With 62 counties, it is the country"s third most populous state. It is bordered by Vermont, Massachusetts, Connecticut, New Jersey, and Pennsylvania, and shares a water border with Rhode Island as well as an international border with the Canadian provinces of Quebec and Ontario. Its five largest cities are New York City, Buffalo, Rochester, Yonkers, and Syracuse.
Society	A society is a grouping of individuals, which is characterized by common interest and may have distinctive culture and institutions.
Historical	((race)) The historical definition of race was an immutable and distinct type or species, sharing distinct racial characteristics such as constitution, temperament, and mental abilities. These races were not conceived as being related with each other, but formed a hierarchy of inherent value called the Great Chain of Being with Europeans usually at the top. As time progressed, Charles Darwin"s theory of evolution was applied to races.

221

Aid	Aid is the help, mostly economic, which may be provided to communities or countries in the event of a humanitarian crisis or to achieve a socioeconomic objective. Humanitarian aid is therefore primarily used for emergency relief, while development aid aims to create long-term sustainable economic growth. Wealthier countries typically provide aid to economically developing countries.
Due process	Basic constitutional principle based on the concept of the primacy of the individual and the complementary concept of limitation on governmental power; safeguards the individual from unfair state procedures in judicial or administrative proceedings; due process rights have been extended to juvenile trials.
Federal government	A federal government is the common government of a federation. The structure of federal government s vary from institution to institution based on a broad definition of a basic federal political system, there are two or more levels of government that exist within an established territory and govern through common institutions with overlapping or shared powers as prescribed by a constitution. · Government of Australia · Government of Belgium · Government of Brazil · Government of Canada · Government of Germany · Government of India · Government of Malaysia · Government of Mexico · Government of Russia · Government of Switzerland · Government of the United States The United States is considered the first modern federation. After declaring independence from Britain, the U.S. adopted its first constitution, the Articles of Confederation in 1781.
Government	A government is a body that has the authority to make and the power to enforce laws within a civil, corporate, religious, academic, or other organization or group.
Court of last resort	In some countries, provinces and states, the court of last resort is the highest court whose rulings cannot be challenged.
United States	The United States is a constitutional federal republic comprising fifty states and a federal district. The country is situated mostly in central North America, where its forty-eight contiguous states and Washington, D.C., the capital district, lie between the Pacific and Atlantic Oceans, bordered by Canada to the north and Mexico to the south.

Evidence-based practice	The term evidence-based practice refers to preferential use of mental and behavioral health interventions for which systematic empirical research has provided evidence of statistically significant effectiveness as treatments for specific problems. It is an approach which tries to specify the way in which professionals or other decision-makers should make decisions by identifying such evidence that there may be for a practice, and rating it according to how scientifically sound it may be. Its goal is to eliminate unsound or excessively risky practices in favour of those that have better outcomes.
Constitution	A constitution is a system, often codified as a written document, that establishes the rules and principles that govern an organization or political entity. In the case of countries, this term refers specifically to a national constitution defining the fundamental political principles, and establishing the structure, procedures, powers and duties, of a government.
Death	Death is the permanent end of the life of a biological organism. Many factors can cause or contribute to it, including predation, disease, habitat destruction, senescence, malnutrition and accidents. The principal causes in developed countries is diseases related to aging.
Death penalty	Death penalty is the execution of a convicted criminal by the state as punishment for crimes known as capital crimes or capital offences. The execution of criminals and political opponents was used by nearly all societies—both to punish crime and to suppress political dissent.
Double jeopardy	Double jeopardy is a procedural defense that forbids a defendant from being tried a second time for the same crime. At common law a defendant can plead autrefois acquit or autrefois convict; meaning the defendant has been acquitted or convicted of the same offense.
Eighth Amendment	The Eighth Amendment Amendment VIII to the United States Constitution, which is part of the United States Bill of Rights, prohibits excessive bail or fines, as well as cruel and unusual punishment. The phrases employed are taken from the English Bill of Rights. The Cruel and Unusual Punishment Clause is the only part of the Amendment that has been made applicable to the states via the Due Process Clause of the Fourteenth Amendment. The Excessive Bail and Excessive Fines Clauses have not been made applicable to the states.
Fifth Amendment	The Fifth Amendment Amendment V of the United States Constitution, which is part of the Bill of Rights, is related to legal procedure. Its guarantees stem from English common law as established by Magna Carta in 1215. For instance, grand juries and the phrase "due process" both trace their origin to the Magna Carta.
McKeiver v. Pennsylvania	McKeiver v. Pennsylvania was a decision of the United States Supreme Court. The Court held that juveniles in juvenile criminal proceedings were not entitled to a jury trial by the Sixth or Fourteenth Amendments. The Court"s plurality opinion left the precise reasoning for the decision unclear [1].Although the right to a jury trial is not guaranteed by the U.S Constitution in these cases, states may, and some do, employ jury trials in juvenile proceedings if they wish to do so.

Thompson v. Oklahoma	Thompson v. Oklahoma was the first case since the moratorium on capital punishment was lifted in the United States in which the U.S. Supreme Court overturned the death sentence of a minor on grounds of "cruel and unusual punishment."
Committee	A committee is a type of small deliberative assembly that is usually subordinate to another, larger deliberative assembly.
Crime	A normative definition views crime as deviant behavior that violates prevailing norms, specifically, cultural standards prescribing how humans ought to behave.
Delinquency Prevention	That which involves any nonjustice program or policy designed to prevent the occurrence of a future delinquent act is referred to as delinquency prevention.
Fourteenth Amendment	The Fourteenth Amendment Amendment XIV to the United States Constitution is one of the post-Civil War amendments known as the Reconstruction Amendments, first intended to secure rights for former slaves. It includes the Due Process and Equal Protection Clauses, among others. It was proposed on June 13, 1866, and was ratified on July 9, 1868. It is perhaps the most significant structural change to the Constitution since the passage of the United States Bill of Rights.
Justice	Justice concerns the proper ordering of things and persons within a society. As a concept it has been subject to philosophical, legal, and theological reflection and debate throughout history.
Juvenile courts	Juvenile courts are courts specifically created and given authority to try and pass judgments for crimes committed by persons who have not attained the age of majority. In most modern legal systems, crimes committed by children and minors are treated differently and differentially regarding the same crimes committed by adults.
Kentucky	Kentucky is a state located in the east central United States of America. Kentucky is normally included in the group of Southern states, but it is sometimes included, geographically and culturally, in the Midwest. Kentucky is one of four U.S. states to be officially known as a commonwealth. Originally a part of Virginia, in 1792 it became the 15th state to join the Union. Kentucky is the 37th largest state in terms of land area, and ranks 26th in population.
Communities	In biological terms, a community is a group of interacting organisms sharing an environment. In human communities, intent, belief, resources, preferences, needs, risks, and a number of other conditions may be present and common, affecting the identity of the participants and their degree of cohesiveness. In sociology, the concept of community has caused infinite debate, and sociologists are yet to reach agreement on a definition of the term.
That	The word That is used in the English language for several grammatical purposes:

	· to introduce a restrictive clause · as a demonstrative pronoun · as a complementizer. In the Old English language That was spelled þæt. It was also abbreviated as a letter Thorn, þ, with the ascender crossed, ê ¥ .
Risk factor	A risk factor is a variable associated with an increased risk of disease or infection. risk factor s are correlational and not necessarily causal, because correlation does not imply causation. For example, being young cannot be said to cause measles, but young people are more at risk as they are less likely to have developed immunity during a previous epidemic.
Authority	In politics, authority is often used interchangeably with the term "power". However, their meanings differ: while "power" refers to the ability to achieve certain ends, "authority" refers to the legitimacy, justification and right to exercise that power. For example, whilst a mob has the power to punish a criminal, such as through lynching, only the courts have the authority to order capital punishment.
Conflict	Conflict is actual or perceived opposition of needs, values and interests. A Conflict can be internal (within oneself) or external (between two or more individuals.) Conflict as a concept can help explain many aspects of social life such as social disagreement, Conflict s of interests, and fights between individuals, groups, or organizations.
Research	Research is defined as human activity based on intellectual application in the investigation of matter. The primary aim for applied research is discovering, interpreting, and the development of methods and systems for the advancement of human knowledge on a wide variety of scientific matters of our world and the universe. Research can use the scientific method, but need not do so.
Child	A child is a boy or girl who has not reached puberty, but also refers to offspring of any age.
Right	In jurisprudence and law, a right is the legal or moral entitlement to do or refrain from doing something or to obtain or refrain from obtaining an action, thing or recognition in civil society. Compare with privilege, or a thing to which one has a just claim. They serve as rules of interaction between people, and, as such, they place constraints and obligations upon the actions of individuals or groups.
Sanction	A punishment for nonconformity that reinforces socially approved forms of behavior is a sanction.In a sociological context, sanction may refer to mechanisms of social control.
Strategy	A Strategy is a long term plan of action designed to achieve a particular goal, most often "winning."

Community	A community is a social group of organisms sharing an environment, normally with shared interests. In human communities, intent, belief, resources, preferences, needs, risks and a number of other conditions may be present and common, affecting the identity of the participants and their degree of cohesiveness.
Community service	Community service refers to service that a person performs for the benefit of his or her local community. People become involved in community service for a range of reasons, for some, it is an altruistic act, for others it is a punishment.
Family	A family consists of a domestic group of people, typically affiliated by birth or marriage, or by analogous or comparable relationships — including domestic partnership, cohabitation, adoption, surname and ownership.
Engagement	An engagement is a promise to marry, and also refers to the time between proposal and marriage.
School	A school is an institution where students learn while under the supervision of teachers. In most systems of formal education, students progress through a series of schools: primary school, secondary school, and possibly a university or vocational school. A school may also be dedicated to one particular field, such as a school of economics or a school of dance.
Female	Female is the sex of an organism, or a part of an organism, which produces ova. The ova are defined as the larger gametes in a heterogamous reproduction system.
Report	In writing, a report is a document characterized by information or other content reflective of inquiry or investigation, which is tailored to the context of a given situation and audience. The purpose of report s is usually to inform. However, report s may include persuasive elements, such as recommendations, suggestions, or other motivating conclusions that indicate possible future actions the report reader might take.
State government	A state government is the government of a subnational entity in states with federal forms of government, which shares political power with the federal government or national government. A state government may have some level of political autonomy, or be subject to the direct control of the federal government.
Mental health	Mental health is a term used to describe either a level of cognitive or emotional wellbeing or an absence of a mental disorder.
Minority	A minority is a sociological group that does not constitute a politically dominant plurality of the total population of a given society. A sociological minority is not necessarily a numerical minority it may include any group that is disadvantaged with respect to a dominant group in terms of social status, education, employment, wealth and political power.

Study Group	A study group is a small group of people who regularly meet to discuss shared fields of study. These groups can be found found in high school and college settings and within companies.
Trend	A trend is something that somehow becomes popular within mainstream society over a long period of time. It is the direction of a sequence of events that has some momentum and durability.
Website	A website (or web site) is a collection of related web pages, images, videos or other digital assets that are addressed with a common domain name or IP address in an Internet Protocol-based network. A web site is hosted on at least one web server, accessible via the Internet or a private local area network. A web page is a document, typically written in plain text interspersed with formatting instructions of Hypertext Markup Language (HTML, XHTML.)
Addiction	A pattern of behavior characterized by an overwhelming involvement with using a drug and securing its supply is defined as an addiction.
Alcohol abuse	Alcohol abuse, as described in the DSM-IV, is a psychiatric diagnosis describing the use of alcoholic beverages despite negative consequences.
Development aid	Development aid is aid given by governmental and economic agencies to support the economic, social and political development of developing countries. It is distinguished from humanitarian aid as being aimed at alleviating poverty in the long term, rather than alleviating suffering in the short term.
Employment	Employment is a contract between two parties, one being the employer and the other being the employee. An employee may be defined as: "A person in the service of another under any contract of hire, express or implied, oral or written, where the employer has the power or right to control and direct the employee in the material details of how the work is to be performed."
American Bar Association	The American Bar Association is a voluntary bar association of lawyers and law students, which is not specific to any jurisdiction in the United States.
Need	A Need is something that is necessary for humans to live a healthy life. Need s are distinguished from wants because a deficiency would cause a clear negative outcome, such as dysfunction or death. Need s can be objective and physical, such as food and water, or they can be subjective and psychological, such as the Need for self-esteem.
From each according to his ability, to each according to his need	From each according to his ability, to each according to his need is a slogan popularized by Karl Marx in his 1875 Critique of the Gotha Program. The phrase summarizes the principles that, under a communist system, every person should contribute to society to the best of his ability and consume from society in proportion to his needs, regardless of how much he has contributed. In the Marxist view, such an arrangement will be made possible by the abundance of goods and services that a developed communist society will produce; the idea is that there will be enough to satisfy everyone"s needs.

Statistics	Statistics is a mathematical science pertaining to the collection, analysis, interpretation, and presentation of data. It is applicable to a wide variety of academic disciplines, from the physical and social sciences to the humanities; it is also used and misused for making informed decisions in all areas of business and government.
Detention	Temporary care of a child alleged to be delinquent who requires secure custody in physically restricting facilities pending court disposition or execution of a court order is detention.
National Council on Crime and Delinquency	The National Council on Crime and Delinquency, founded in 1907, is a nonprofit organization that promotes effective, humane, fair, and economically sound solutions to family, community, and justice problems. The group conducts research, promotes reform initiatives, and seeks to work with individuals, public and private organizations, and the media to prevent and reduce crime and delinquency.
Substance abuse	Substance abuse refers to the overindulgence in and dependence on a psychoactive leading to effects that are detrimental to the individual"s physical health or mental health, or the welfare of others.
School violence	School violence refers to violence and crime taking place within educational institutions.
Student	A student could be described as "one who directs zeal at a subject".
Bullying	Bullying is the act of intentionally causing harm to others through verbal harassment, physical assault, or other more subtle methods of coercion such as manipulation.
Teacher	In education, a teacher is one who helps students or pupils, often in a school, as well as in a family, religious or community setting.
Word	A Word is the smallest free form (an item that may be uttered in isolation with semantic or pragmatic content) in a language, in contrast to a morpheme, which is the smallest unit of meaning. A Word may consist of only one morpheme (e.g. cat), but a single morpheme may not be able to exist as a free form . Typically, a Word will consist of a root or stem, and zero or more affixes.
Department of Education	The United States Department of Education is a Cabinet-level department of the United States government. Created by the Department of Education Organization Act. It began operating in 1980.
Judge	A judge is an official who presides over a court. The powers, functions, method of appointment, discipline, and training of a judge vary widely across different jurisdictions.
United States Department of Education	The United States Department of Education a Cabinet-level department of the United States government. It"s primary function is to formulate federal funding programs involving education and to enforce federal educational laws regarding privacy and civil rights.
Protocol	In international politics, Protocol is the etiquette of diplomacy and affairs of state.

A Protocol is a rule which guides how an activity should be performed, especially in the field of diplomacy. In diplomatic services and governmental fields of endeavor protocols are often unwritten guidelines.

Professional	A professional can be either a person in a profession or in sports for payment.
Association	Association in archaeology has more than one meaning and is confusing to the layman. Archaeology has been critiqued as a soft science with a somewhat poor standardization of terms. Associated finds or objects refers to a close relationship between two or more objects.
Ethics	Ethics, a major branch of philosophy, is the study of values and customs of a person or group. It covers the analysis and employment of concepts such as right and wrong, good and evil, and responsibility. It is divided into three primary areas: meta-ethics, normative ethics, and applied ethics.
Social	Social refers to human society or its organization. Although the term is a crucial category in social science and often used in public discourse, its meaning is at times vague, suggesting that it is a fuzzy concept. An added difficulty is that social attributes or relationships may not be directly observable and visible, and must be inferred by abstract thought.
Client	In ancient Roman society, a Client was a plebeian who was sponsored by a patron benefactor . The patron assisted his Client with his protection and regular gifts; the Client dedicated his vote whenever the patron or his associate was up for election. This right of patronage was established by Romulus, to unite the plebians and the patricians together, in such a manner that one might live without envy, and the other without contempt.

Procedure	In all lawsuits involving Conflict of Laws, questions of Procedure as opposed to substance are always determined by the lex fori, i.e. the law of the state in which the case is being litigated.
	This is a part of the process called characterisation. Issues identified as procedural include the following:
	
	· By initiating the action before the forum court, the plaintiff is asking for the grant of the local remedies. This will not be a problem so long as the form of the relief is broadly similar to the relief available under the lex causae, i.e. the law selected under the choice of law rules. But forum courts may refuse a remedy in two situations:
	    if the effect of granting the relief sought would offend against the public policy of the forum court;
	    if the effect of the relief would be so different from that available under the lex causae that it makes the right sought to be enforced a different right. For example, in English law, the court was asked in Phrantzes v Argenti 2 QB 19 to enforce a Greek marriage dowry agreement.

Internet	The Internet is a global system of interconnected computer networks that interchange data by packet switching using the standardized Internet Protocol Suite. It is a "network of networks" that consists of millions of private and public, academic, business, and government networks of local to global scope that are linked by copper wires, fiber-optic cables, wireless connections, and other technologies.

The Internet carries various information resources and services, such as electronic mail, online chat, file transfer and file sharing, online gaming, and the inter-linked hypertext documents and other resources of the World Wide Web.

Malpractice

In law, malpractice is a type of tort in which the misfeasance, malfeasance or nonfeasance of a professional, under a duty to act, fails to follow generally accepted professional standards, and that breach of duty is the proximate cause of injury to a plaintiff who suffers damages.

Liability

Anything that is a hindrance or puts individuals at a disadvantage is considered a liability.

Lesbian

A lesbian is a woman who is romantically and sexually attracted only to other women. Some women in same-sex relationships do not identify as lesbian, but as bisexual, queer, or another label. As with any interpersonal activity, sexual expression depends on the context of the relationship.

Informed consent

Informed consent is a legal condition whereby a person can be said to have given consent based upon an appreciation and understanding of the facts and implications of an action. The individual needs to be in possession of relevant facts and also of his reasoning faculties, such as not being mentally retarded or mentally ill and without an impairment of judgment at the time of consenting.

Confidentiality

Confidentiality has been defined by the International Organization for Standardization as "ensuring that information is accessible only to those authorized to have access" and is one of the cornerstones of Information security. Confidentiality is one of the design goals for many cryptosystems, made possible in practice by the techniques of modern cryptography.

Privilege

A Privilege etymologically "private law" or law relating to a specific individual--is a special entitlement or immunity granted by a government or other authority to a restricted group, either by birth or on a conditional basis. A Privilege can be revoked in some cases. In modern democracies, a Privilege is conditional and granted only after birth.

Child

A child is a boy or girl who has not reached puberty, but also refers to offspring of any age.

Other

The Other or constitutive Other (also referred to as Other ing) is a key concept in continental philosophy, opposed to the Same. It refers, or attempts to refer, to that which is Other than the concept being considered. The term often means a person Other than oneself, and is often capitalised.

Delinquent

Delinquent means one who fails to do that which is required by law or by duty when such failure is minor in nature.

Research

Research is defined as human activity based on intellectual application in the investigation of matter. The primary aim for applied research is discovering, interpreting, and the development of methods and systems for the advancement of human knowledge on a wide variety of scientific matters of our world and the universe. Research can use the scientific method, but need not do so.

Self care	Self care is personal health maintenance.
Environment	The social environment is the identical or similar social positions and social roles as a whole that influence the individuals of a group. The social environment of an individual is the culture that he or she was educated and/or lives in, and the people and institutions with whom the person interacts. A given social environment is likely to create a feeling of solidarity amongst its members, who are more likely to keep together, trust and help one another. Members of the same social environment will often think in similar styles and patterns even when their conclusions differ.
Managed care	The term "managed care" is used to describe a variety of techniques intended to reduce the cost of providing health benefits and improve the quality of care "managed care techniques", organizations that use those techniques or provide them as services to other organizations "managed care organizations", or systems of financing and delivering health care to enrollees organized around managed care techniques and concepts "managed care delivery systems". According to the National Library of Medicine,
Duty	Duty is a term that conveys a sense of moral commitment to someone or something.
Report	In writing, a report is a document characterized by information or other content reflective of inquiry or investigation, which is tailored to the context of a given situation and audience. The purpose of report s is usually to inform. However, report s may include persuasive elements, such as recommendations, suggestions, or other motivating conclusions that indicate possible future actions the report reader might take.
Child Protective Services	Child Protective Services is the name of a governmental agency in many states in the United States that responds to allegations of child abuse or neglect.
Family	A family consists of a domestic group of people, typically affiliated by birth or marriage, or by analogous or comparable relationships — including domestic partnership, cohabitation, adoption, surname and ownership.
Forensic social work	Forensic social work is the application of social work to questions and issues relating to law and legal systems. This specialty of the social work profession goes far beyond clinics and psychiatric hospitals for criminal defendants being evaluated and treated on issues of competency and responsibility. A broader definition includes social work practice which in any way is related to legal issues and litigation, both criminal and civil.

Assessment	Educational Assessment is the process of documenting, usually in measurable terms, knowledge, skills, attitudes and beliefs. Assessment can focus on the individual learner, the learning community (class, workshop, or other organized group of learners), the institution, or the educational system as a whole. According to the Academic Exchange Quarterly: "Studies of a theoretical or empirical nature (including case studies, portfolio studies, exploratory, or experimental work) addressing the Assessment of learner aptitude and preparation, motivation and learning styles, learning outcomes in achievement and satisfaction in different educational contexts are all welcome, as are studies addressing issues of measurable standards and benchmarks".
Child advocacy	Child advocacy refers to a range of individuals, professionals and advocacy organizations who promote the optimal development of children. An individual or organization engaging in advocacy typically seeks to protect children"s rights which may be abridged or abused in a number of areas. Rights can be divided into two categories: negative (rights to be free from) and positive (rights to).
Justice	Justice concerns the proper ordering of things and persons within a society. As a concept it has been subject to philosophical, legal, and theological reflection and debate throughout history.
Policy	A policy is a deliberate plan of action to guide decisions and achieve rational outcomes. The term may apply to government, private sector organizations and groups, and individuals. Presidential executive orders, corporate privacy policies, and parliamentary rules of order are all examples of policy. Policy differs from rules or law. While law can compel or prohibit behaviors policy merely guides actions toward those that are most likely to achieve a desired outcome.
Structured interview	A structured interview is a quantitative research method commonly employed in survey research. The aim of this approach is to ensure that each interviewee is presented with exactly the same questions in the same order. This ensures that answers can be reliably aggregated and that comparisons can be made with confidence between sample subgroups or between different survey periods.
Adoption	Adoption is the legal act of permanently placing a child with a parent or parents other than the birth mother or father. An adoption order has the effect of severing the parental responsibilities and rights of the birth parents and transferring those responsibilities and rights onto the adoptive parents.
Cooperation	Cooperation is the practice of individuals or larger societal entities working in common with mutually agreed-upon goals and possibly methods, instead of working separately in competition, and in which the success of one is dependent and contingent upon the success of another.
Convention	A convention is a set of agreed, stipulated or generally accepted social norms, norms, standards or criteria, often taking the form of a custom.

Court	A court is a public forum used by a power base to adjudicate disputes and dispense civil, labor, administrative and criminal justice under its laws. In common law and civil law states, courts are the central means for dispute resolution, and it is generally understood that all persons have an ability to bring their claims before a court. Similarly, those accused of a crime have the right to present their defense before a court.
International adoption	International adoption is a type of adoption in which an individual or couple becomes the legal and permanent parents of a child born in another country. In general, prospective adoptive parents must meet the legal adoption requirements of their country of residence and those of the country in which the child was born.
Legal rights	Legal rights refrain from doing something or to obtain or refrain from obtaining an action, thing or recognition in civil society. Compare with duty, referring to behavior that is expected or required of the citizen, and with privilege, referring to something that can be conferred and revoked.
Nation	A Nation is a body of people who share a real or imagined common history, culture, language or ethnic origin, who typically inhabit a particular country or territory. The development and conceptualization of the Nation is closely related to the development of modern industrial states and Nation alist movements in Europe in the 18th and 19th centuries, although Nation alists would trace Nation s into the past along an uninterrupted lines of historical narrative. Benedict Anderson argued that Nation s were "imagined communities" because "the members of even the smallest Nation will never know most of their fellow-members, meet them, or even hear of them, yet in the minds of each lives the image of their communion", and traced their origins back to vernacular print journalism, which by its very nature was limited with linguistic zones and addressed a common audience.
Respect	Respect is the acknowledgment that someone or something has value.
Right	In jurisprudence and law, a right is the legal or moral entitlement to do or refrain from doing something or to obtain or refrain from obtaining an action, thing or recognition in civil society. Compare with privilege, or a thing to which one has a just claim. They serve as rules of interaction between people, and, as such, they place constraints and obligations upon the actions of individuals or groups.
Court of last resort	In some countries, provinces and states, the court of last resort is the highest court whose rulings cannot be challenged.
United Nations	The United Nations is an international organization whose stated aims are to facilitate cooperation in international law, international security, economic development, social progress and human rights issues.

Public education	Public education refers to schooling mandated for or offered to all children by the government, whether national, regional provided by an institution of civil government, and paid for, in whole or in part, by taxes. The term is generally applied to basic education, including kindergarten to twelfth grade (K-12) education, also referred to as primary and secondary education. Public education can also be post-secondary education, advanced education colleges, or technical schools funded and overseen by government rather than private entities.
Planning	Planning in organizations and public policy is both the organizational process of creating and maintaining a plan; and the psychological process of thinking about the activities required to create a desired future on some scale.
Welfare	Welfare is financial assistance paid by taxpayers to people who are unable to support themselves. Some welfare is general, while specific and can only be invoked under certain circumstances, such as a scholarship. Individuals may apply for welfare due to disability, lack of education or job training, a low demand for unskilled labor, substance abuse, or an unwillingness to work.
Organization	In sociology organization is understood as planned, coordinated and purposeful action of human beings to construct or compile a common tangible or intangible product or service.
Education	Education encompasses teaching and learning specific skills, and also something less tangible but more profound: the imparting of knowledge, positive judgement and well-developed wisdom. Education has as one of its fundamental aspects the imparting of culture from generation to generation.
Family preservation	Family preservation was the movement to help keep children at home with their families rather than in foster homes or institutions. This movement was a reaction to the earlier policy of family breakup, which pulled children out of unfit homes. Extreme poverty alone was seen as a justified reason to remove children.
Foster care	Foster care is a system by which a certified, stand-in "parent" cares for minor children or young peoples who have been removed from their birth parents or other custodial adults by state authority. Responsibility for the young person is assumed by the relevant governmental authority and a placement with another family found. There can be voluntary placements by a parent of a child into foster care.
Minor	In law, the term minor is used to refer to a person who is under the age in which one legally assumes adulthood and is legally granted rights afforded to adults in society. Depending on the jurisdiction and application, this age may vary, but is usually marked at either 18 or 21. Specifically, the status of "minor" is defined by the age of majority[

Mobilization	Mobilization is the act of assembling and making both troops and supplies ready for war. The word mobilization was first used, in a military context, in order to describe the preparation of the Prussian army during the 1850s and 1860s. Mobilization theories and techniques have continuously changed since then.
Poverty	Poverty may be seen as the collective condition of poor people, or of poor groups, and in this sense entire nation-states are sometimes regarded as poor. Although the most severe poverty is in the developing world, there is evidence of poverty in every region.
Youth	Youth is defined by as, "The time of life when one is young; especially: a: the period between childhood and maturity b: the early period of existence, growth, or development."
Historical	((race)) The historical definition of race was an immutable and distinct type or species, sharing distinct racial characteristics such as constitution, temperament, and mental abilities. These races were not conceived as being related with each other, but formed a hierarchy of inherent value called the Great Chain of Being with Europeans usually at the top. As time progressed, Charles Darwin"s theory of evolution was applied to races.
Federal government	A federal government is the common government of a federation. The structure of federal government s vary from institution to institution based on a broad definition of a basic federal political system, there are two or more levels of government that exist within an established territory and govern through common institutions with overlapping or shared powers as prescribed by a constitution. · Government of Australia · Government of Belgium · Government of Brazil · Government of Canada · Government of Germany · Government of India · Government of Malaysia · Government of Mexico · Government of Russia · Government of Switzerland · Government of the United States The United States is considered the first modern federation. After declaring independence from Britain, the U.S. adopted its first constitution, the Articles of Confederation in 1781.
Government	A government is a body that has the authority to make and the power to enforce laws within a civil, corporate, religious, academic, or other organization or group.

Moral	A moral is a message conveyed or a lesson to be learned from a story or event. The moral may be left to the hearer, reader or viewer to determine for themselves, or may be explicitly encapsulated in a maxim.
Morale	Morale is an intangible term used for the capacity of people to maintain belief in an institution or a goal, or even in oneself and others. The second term applies particularly to military personnel and to members of sports teams, but is also applicable in business and in any other organizational context, particularly in times of stress or controversy.
United States	The United States is a constitutional federal republic comprising fifty states and a federal district. The country is situated mostly in central North America, where its forty-eight contiguous states and Washington, D.C., the capital district, lie between the Pacific and Atlantic Oceans, bordered by Canada to the north and Mexico to the south.
Abortion	An abortion is the removal or expulsion of an embryo or fetus from the uterus, resulting in or caused by its death. This can occur spontaneously as a miscarriage or be artificially induced by chemical, surgical or other means.
Due process	Basic constitutional principle based on the concept of the primacy of the individual and the complementary concept of limitation on governmental power; safeguards the individual from unfair state procedures in judicial or administrative proceedings; due process rights have been extended to juvenile trials.
State government	A state government is the government of a subnational entity in states with federal forms of government, which shares political power with the federal government or national government. A state government may have some level of political autonomy, or be subject to the direct control of the federal government.
Importance	Importance is an idea that has existed forever but is being applied very differently in the internet age. It"s a simple cave rules notion relating to ones contribution to a community create some form of their importance in the community. It is the essence of why sites like Wikipedia work.
Advocatus	An Advocatus was generally a medieval term meaning "lawyer". The term was also used in continental Europe as the title of the lay lord charged with the protection and representation in secular matters of an abbey, known more fully as an Advocatus ecclesiae. The office is traceable as early as the beginning of the 5th century in the Roman Empire, the churches being allowed to choose defensores from the body of advocates to represent them in the courts.
Sanction	A punishment for nonconformity that reinforces socially approved forms of behavior is a sanction.In a sociological context, sanction may refer to mechanisms of social control.
Software	Computer software, or just software is a general term used to describe a collection of computer programs, procedures and documentation that perform some tasks on a computer system. A screenshot of the OpenOffice.org Writer desktop software

The term includes:

· Application software such as word processors which perform productive tasks for users,
· System software such as operating systems, which interface with hardware to provide the necessary services for application software, and
· Middleware which controls and co-ordinates distributed systems.
Software includes websites, programs, video games etc. that are coded by programming languages like C, C++, etc.

· Firmware which is software programmed resident to electrically programmable memory devices on board mainboards or other types of integrated hardware carriers
· Testware which is an umbrella term or container term for all utilities and application software that serve in combination for testing a software package but not necessarily may optionally contribute to operational purposes. As such, testware is not a standing configuration but merely a working environment for application software or subsets thereof.
"Software" is sometimes used in a broader context to mean anything which is not hardware but which is used with hardware, such as film, tapes and records.
Computer software is often regarded as anything but hardware, meaning that the "hard" are the parts that are tangible while the "soft" part is the intangible objects inside the computer.

Trend	A trend is something that somehow becomes popular within mainstream society over a long period of time. It is the direction of a sequence of events that has some momentum and durability.
Website	A website (or web site) is a collection of related web pages, images, videos or other digital assets that are addressed with a common domain name or IP address in an Internet Protocol-based network. A web site is hosted on at least one web server, accessible via the Internet or a private local area network. A web page is a document, typically written in plain text interspersed with formatting instructions of Hypertext Markup Language (HTML, XHTML.)
American Academy of Pediatrics	The American Academy of Pediatrics is an organization of pediatricians, physicians trained to deal with the medical care of infants, children, and adolescents. It is a partner in the Campaign for Children"s Health Care, a multi-year campaign to raise awareness about the problem of uninsured children in America.
Detention	Temporary care of a child alleged to be delinquent who requires secure custody in physically restricting facilities pending court disposition or execution of a court order is detention.
Human	A Human is a member of a species of bipedal primates in the family Hominidae . DNA and fossil evidence indicates that modern Human s originated in east Africa about 200,000 years ago. When compared to other animals and primates, Human s have a highly developed brain, capable of abstract reasoning, language, introspection and problem solving.

Public	Public is about the what of belonging to the people; relating to, or affecting, a nation, state, or community; opposed to private; as, the public treasury, a road or lake. Public is also defined as the people of a nation not affiliated with the government of that nation.
Statistics	Statistics is a mathematical science pertaining to the collection, analysis, interpretation, and presentation of data. It is applicable to a wide variety of academic disciplines, from the physical and social sciences to the humanities; it is also used and misused for making informed decisions in all areas of business and government.
Study Group	A study group is a small group of people who regularly meet to discuss shared fields of study. These groups can be found found in high school and college settings and within companies.
Abuse	Abuse refers to the use or treatment of something that is seen as harmful. The term can be used for anything ranging from the misuse of a piece of equipment to the severe maltreatment of a person.
Accountability	Accountability is a concept in ethics with several meanings. It is often used synonymously with such concepts as answerability, enforcement, responsibility, blameworthiness, liability and other terms associated with the expectation of account-giving.
Analysis	Analysis is the process of breaking a complex topic or substance into smaller parts to gain a better understanding of it. The technique has been applied in the study of mathematics and logic since before Aristotle, though analysis as a formal concept is a relatively recent development. As a formal concept, the method has variously been ascribed by Ibn al-Haytham, Descartes, Galileo, and Isaac Newton, as a practical method of physical discovery.
Cultural Competence	Cultural competence refers to an ability to interact effectively with people of different cultures.
Data Analysis	Qualitative data analysis QDA or qualitative research is the analysis of non-numerical data, for example words, photographs, observations, etc..
Department of Education	The United States Department of Education is a Cabinet-level department of the United States government. Created by the Department of Education Organization Act. It began operating in 1980.
Engagement	An engagement is a promise to marry, and also refers to the time between proposal and marriage.
Government Accountability Office	The Government Accountability Office is the audit, evaluation, and investigative arm of the United States Congress. It is located in the Legislative branch of the United States government.
Resource	A resource is any physical or virtual entity of limited availability, or anything used to help one earn a living. In most cases, commercial or even ethic factors require resource allocation through resource management. As resource s are very useful, we attach some information value to them.

School	A school is an institution where students learn while under the supervision of teachers. In most systems of formal education, students progress through a series of schools: primary school, secondary school, and possibly a university or vocational school. A school may also be dedicated to one particular field, such as a school of economics or a school of dance.
Social Work	Social work is a helping profession focused on social change, problem solving in human relationships and the empowerment and liberation of people to enhance well-being.
Substance Abuse	Substance abuse refers to the overindulgence in and dependence on a psychoactive leading to effects that are detrimental to the individual"s physical health or mental health, or the welfare of others.
United States Department of Education	The United States Department of Education a Cabinet-level department of the United States government. It"s primary function is to formulate federal funding programs involving education and to enforce federal educational laws regarding privacy and civil rights.
U.S. Government	The U.S. government is the governmental body that carries out the roles assigned to the federation of individual states established by the Constitution. The federal government has three branches: the executive, legislative, and judicial. Through a system of separation of powers or "checks and balances," each of these branches has some authority to act on its own, some authority to regulate the other two branches, and has some of its own authority, in turn, regulated by the other branches.

CPSIA information can be obtained
at www.ICGtesting.com
Printed in the USA
BVHW011134090122
625806BV00024B/388